The Adult Baby's Guidebook

The life challenges of the perpetually diapered

Brian Burch

ISBN-13: 978-1503257351

ISBN-10: 1503257355

Introduction

This is a book about acceptance. Each section illustrates a different form of acceptance. Acceptance is the key to happiness, and resistance the cause of all misery.

*   *   *

I was 3 years old and potty trained, but I'd just woken up from the most amazing dream ever! I was a tiny little monkey in an empty wading pool along with about 10 other little monkeys. We were all wearing diapers. I didn't care that I was a monkey. I could fit into baby diapers! I wanted that dream to last forever. I was so disappointed when I woke up. I tried to go back to sleep so the dream could continue, but to no avail. Every night for at least the next two years, I'd think about that dream as I was falling asleep, hoping I could have that dream again. I never did. I craved - desperately, you could say - to be back in diapers again. That was at age three. I'm 33 now, and that desire to wear diapers has never left me, nor has it waned.

Through my adolescence, this inclination brought with it many side effects. I was socially awkward, to start. I did not love or respect myself. On the contrary, I considered myself a freak of nature, the only weirdo in the world that liked diapers. I was alone, did not fit in, was unwelcome in society. Nobody could ever understand me or love me.

What was I to do? Stop wearing diapers? Not that easy. Believe me, I tried. I prayed and prayed to be normal. I quit diapers countless times, begging God to give me the strength to stay away, but it would only be a matter of weeks before the need overwhelmed me and I'd sneak another diaper out of the baby's closet.

I learned around age 15 or so that I was not the only person in the world with an infatuation with diapers. That was a problem, though. The first 15 years of my life I held the firm belief that I was different than everyone else in the world in a bad way. Already, my foundation for a mentally healthy lifestyle was unstable. Even after I had learned there were others, I did not realize the damage already done, nor the life I was heading into. My adolescence was rough, but my teenage years got worse, and my adult life worse still.

But what did I expect? Someone to talk to? Someone who could understand me and guide me through the foreign territory that is life as an Adult Baby? I couldn't just tell my best friend I was into diapers. That's not the sort of thing you can tell people. You're a freak, living in a world full of normal people, in which you are forced to act normal.

Fast forward to age thirty, when I finally become fed up with my repetitive and unfulfilling patterns, and I began to actively seek answers. Since then, I have learned to be happy, to love myself, and to find my place in this world being different than everyone else. I am 100% certain that I am not the only person that grew up with these experiences of self-hatred based on a strange desire. I thought to myself that there should be a guidebook for people like us. But there's not... until now!

*   *   *

You see, there are many Adult Babies (AB) and so called Diaper Lovers (DL) in the world (collectively, the ABDL community). There are hundreds of websites devoted to pictures of sexy people in diapers, chat rooms and forums about what is the best and most babyish diaper on the market, etc. Very few, if any, talk in depth about what it's like living as an AB/DL in a non-AB/DL world, and the unique struggles we face. I'm not just talking about the awkward diaper change in the mall's bathroom stall. I'm talking about how to tell your girlfriend that you wear diapers, and how to love yourself when you know you're different than everyone. I'm talking about finding your worth in the world.

The AB/DL community needs a leader that will help these innocent, confused people. I needed that help when I was young, and never received it. I think I never received it because it was simply not available.

If you're looking for a sexy story about a sorority that kidnapped and diapered an innocent freshman jock on his way to football practice, this is not your book. There are plenty of diaper erotica stories on Amazon. This book is intended to be a guidebook for those that genuinely want to know how to navigate the life of an Adult Baby or Diaper Lover. Whether you are an AB/DL, or you think you are; or your spouse or child is into diapers, or you think they are; or maybe you're just curious about the lifestyle of an Adult Baby, this is the guidebook for you all.

*   *   *

I write most of this book as if I were writing a letter to my younger self. I struggled throughout much of my teens and twenties, followed by a great leap of self-discovery at age thirty. I chose to write this handbook of sorts that, I believe, would have helped me greatly to have had in my possession at age fifteen. This rings especially true for section 3, which might as well start with "Dear fifteen year old Brian." Section 4 might as well start with "Dear fifteen year old Brian's parents." I have no doubt whatsoever that there are other people of all ages in the same situation I was in at age fifteen, hence the necessity of this book. If I've spent the last few months working on this book and it makes a positive difference in only one person's life, I will call it a success.

Because this book is geared towards my younger self, I will make some generalizations up front, and a disclaimer that it does not have to affect you. I will refer to the Adult Baby in this book as a male, not because all Adult Babies are males, and not because the information in this book applies only to males, but because it's far easier to communicate using one pronoun instead of two, and I chose he because I am a he.

*   *   *

Adult Babies are different. We are a strange folk. Wearing a diaper is a rare quirk. While I speak from the perspective of an Adult Baby, and refer to my specific quirk often, there is no reason this book can't apply to anyone with any other quirk. Replace the word "diaper" with "panties" or "pirate clothes" and it would read essentially the same.

My point is that the information in this book is entirely valuable not just to Adult Babies in diapers, but to anyone that feels a little different. That is to say, this book can apply, on one level or another, to everyone.

We, as humans, are far more similar and connected than we recognize.

*   *   *

This brings me to my final note before we get into the bulk of matter: God. I refer to God a few times in this book, but I want to be clear - as clear as possible, anyway - about to what, exactly, I am referring to.

In section 2, when I refer to God, I am talking about the Christian God. During that time in my life, I was Christian, and when I say that I prayed to God, I was praying to the God of the Bible.

Through the rest of the book, I refer to God in a different way, though.

Life is one of the most mysterious things in the universe. What makes me who I am? And you who you are? What made Hitler and Einstein who they were? The debate between nature vs. nurture fails to address a key piece of the puzzle, the very life force within us that gives us life.

We should consider a physical law that life only comes from life. It's experimentally true. We've never seen life come from non-life, nor will we ever. There is something beyond what we see and experience in this physical world that makes us who we are.

In this way, we are connected to a realm beyond the physical. That we all are connected to the realm, that which gives us life, is what we all have in common. The life-force is what I refer to when I refer to God in this book. You can call it the life-force, the universe, Mother Nature, God, Allah, or whatever else you want to call it, yet this is only a matter of semantics.

I do not ask you to believe in any dogmatic character. I only refer to the magical essence that makes you alive and gives you purpose in this world. Feel free to call it what you want, but I urge you not to refute the message because you are uncomfortable with the word I use. The advice herein applies to all, regardless of religion.

When I say "God", I refer to the non-physical, albeit natural, forces in our lives.

*   *   *

My expertise on the subject of Adult Babies is first hand. I am not a doctor, psychiatrist, psychologist, or trained counselor. I give this information as someone with the experience of being a lifelong AB/DL. I offer the inspiration as someone who's grown from a confused, lost AB to a confident, self-loving AB. I have an understanding of ABs, DLs, their challenges, and the community and lifestyle that no doctor ever could. Unless, of course, the doctor was an AB, too. You never know...

Section 1:
What is an Adult Baby?

THE MYTHS

Ask the average person "what is an Adult Baby" and many descriptions come to mind.

-They wear diapers.
-They act like babies.
-They drink out of bottles.
-They suck on pacifiers.
-They're men.
-They're homosexual.
-They talk like babies, i.e. "goo-goo, ga-ga."
-They have mommies or daddies to take care of them, feed them, change them, etc.
-They couldn't possibly handle an adult life.
-They're freaks!
-Perverts!
-Pedophiles!
-They "get off" on walking around in their own feces all day.

WHAT *IS* AN ADULT BABY?

The fact is, adult babies are - get ready - people! The *one* thing they all have in common is that they are people, just like you and me. People are different. There are no two people that are the same. Some like hockey, others like football. Others have no interest in sports at all. Some enjoy tacos, some salads, etc. Also, some people prefer diapers to traditional underwear. Some people identify as an age they are officially not. Many AB's are really nice people. Some are total jerks! It's much like the general population. This is but a subcategory of the population, after all.

My point in all of this is that we can't generalize an Adult Baby any more than we can generalize any other segment of the population. If you think of Adult Babies being separate from society, stop. Society is made up of individuals, and each individual carries with him or her a specific set of characteristics unmatched by any other.

BUT REALLY, WHAT *IS* AN ADULT BABY?

There is much discussion even in the Adult Baby/Diaper Lover (ABDL) community about what it means. There is no official definition of an Adult Baby. While many of the characteristics listed above do apply to many of the members, many do not. Each Adult Baby is different.

The Diaper Lover part is easier to define as an interest in diapers, but even this can mean multiple things. Do they wear diapers? Use them? For what? And so on. Also, I reserve *love* for people, and as such have always felt uncomfortable "loving" any inanimate object. I love my family. I like diapers. However, the term is established, and I will continue to use it to define this subsection of the population, of which I am a part.

Would it surprise you to know that some people like to wear diapers and have no interest in "age-play?" Or that others identify as a toddler but have no interest in diapers? Among those that do wear diapers, some use them partially (#1 but not #2), while others use them to their full capacity, while still others don't use them for the intended purpose at all! Some identify as babies, others as toddlers, and others as older kids, teens, adults, whatever. Some like bottles, some don't. Some like baby clothes, others don't. Do you see my point? We're all different. God doesn't work with a cookie cutter. We each have our own recipe.

The term ABDL, as well as its scientific term, infantilism, is a blanket term describing all or any of the above.

Knowing this, it is important not to make generalizations or assumptions about an Adult Baby. People in my past have assumed that since I'm an Adult Baby, I must be gay, I must be a child molester, and I must walk around carrying a stinky load in my pants. These aren't just wrong, they're harmful. While those of us most aware already know the harm of assumptions and generalizations, many of us fall in the traps of generalizing groups we do not fully understand. I am not talking about Adult Babies specifically here. I am talking about people! And remember, Adult Babies are people. You can trust me. I am one. (Of each!)

Upon discovering one enjoys wearing diapers, you cannot jump to the conclusion that he identifies as a baby or toddler, nor can you jump to the conclusion that he uses said diapers, and you especially can't assume their a pedophile or sick in the head. We are all different.

It is unknown how one becomes an Adult Baby. Some Adult Babies know the source of their desires, I'm sure. I've heard stories of people consciously deciding to try on a diaper and enjoying it. That's not who I'm talking about. It's unknown how some people seem to have the craving to wear diapers sewn into their being. I think it is unknown because people expect such a strange thing to be caused by one specific event in our past. This is not real life.

For me, I have been drawn towards diapers for as long as I can remember. My earliest memory is at age three, dreaming of wearing diapers again. It's possible, I suppose, that this dream was so pleasurable that it began my obsession over diapers. However, I seem to remember that the dream was an expression of my desires already present in my life. An AB friend of mine tells me that he started wondering about diapers when he was thirteen, and, upon sneaking some diapers out of his younger cousin's diaper bag, discovered he really enjoyed it. Now, twenty years later, he's in the same AB club as I. Others date someone else that's an AB as an adult and discover then that they, too, enjoy the lifestyle. For me, it was ingrained in my being from a young age. It's hard for me to imagine others that made a conscious choice to join into the ABDL community. Why someone would choose such a difficult lifestyle is beyond me, but it might not be so difficult if it were more of a choice.

I can tell you my interests and experiences, and I do so in the next section, but it's important that we not define all AB's through me. I do not represent the entire community. I am only me. Nor should your experience with another AB affect your thoughts towards me. In the end, there is little connection amongst all Adult Babies aside from general babyish interests. No one person could possibly represent the "typical" Adult Baby.

Another interesting trend in the community is the abundance of overlapping kinks. Many ABs are also furries, cross-dressers, and into the BDSM scene. Some men identify as baby boys, others as baby girls. Some women identify as baby boys, and others as baby girls.

I do believe that there is a higher percentage of homosexuals in the ABDL community than in society as a whole. Why that would be, I do not know. Also, that's a pure guess based solely on my experience. No official scientific studies have been performed on this topic. Of course, it is inappropriate to make any assumptions regarding any individual of his sexuality based on being an Adult Baby.

IS IT SEXUAL?

For some, yes. For others, no. For some, both.

Many ABs and DLs make it their sole purpose in life to brag that they are pure ABDLs and do not get any sexual gratification from diapers or babyhood. They, in fact, tend to distance themselves from those "freaky sexualized ABDLs", as they feel like that subculture gives all ABDLs a bad name.

For me, it is complicated. I was into diapers when I was three. Can you have a sexual fetish at age three? Is it fair to call it a fetish that young? I was a late developer sexually, not hitting puberty until around fifteen or so. Up until then, was it sexual? I'd say no, but who could be sure? Freud would likely disagree with me, but he'd sexualize a pebble. At fifteen, diapers most certainly became sexualized. I think it is only natural that as one begins puberty, a prominent taboo that is centered around the genitals is bound to be a significant factor in one's sexual maturation. It's important to consider that my sexuality became a part of my desire for diapers, rather than vice versa. Diapers, most certainly, came first. My sexuality evolved to adapt.

Personally, it's now both sexual and non-sexual. There are many aspects of wearing diapers that are entirely enjoyable and completely sexuality-free. There are other aspects of wearing diapers from which I do get sexual pleasure. In addition, I'm entirely capable of having a healthy sex life without the involvement of diapers. Diapers within my sex life sure are fun, though.

I have one AB friend that once tried involving sex with his Adult Baby life, and it rubbed him the wrong way. Being one that identified as a toddler, he vowed to never have a sexual experience again. This is quite common. Others, however, ONLY play diapers and age-play games in a bedroom/sexual setting.

PREDOMINANTLY MEN?

Maybe.

You poor readers. You picked this book up hoping for the straight facts, and all you get is this philosophical gray area.

I was born recently, in 1980. My experience is limited, but here it is.

In the 1990s, when I first discovered the ABDL scene, it was predominately male. The central online site for the ABDL community was DPF.com, which stood for Diaper Pail Friends. It is my estimation that the male to female ratio of this website was near 50:1, and maybe as high as 100:1.

However, this is not a fair representation of the population at large. For one, women tend to take on an amount of abuse online. If a woman enters a group with the 50:1 ratio, she will most certainly get bombarded by emails from AB men interested in her, which can be threatening to a woman, and could easily drive her away.

Another reason may be that a woman acting childish is not as culturally shocking as a man acting childish, and therefore finds personal partners more easily as it gives her less of a complex, thus lessening her need or desire to be included in any groups that will understand her, as she is already accepted by her partner.

In real life gatherings, the ratio split doesn't seem nearly as severe. AB girls I've talked to contribute this to men preferring online interaction to live out their fantasies, and women preferring to interact in real life and forge more meaningful relationships.

There are also developmental and cultural differences that contribute to the split. An active member of a popular internet forum contributed a feminist perspective on the issue. In her comments, she wrote:

> "In patriarchal culture women are already rewarded for playing the "little girl" role a lot of the time, so they're less likely to internalize/fetishize those roles. Men are punished for anything perceived as passive or not fitting in to the role of being a man, so wanting to play out/act little goes against social norms and is

more likely to lead to internalizing those feelings. So a woman who plays at being little has a "sexy" cultural capital that a man doesn't, which leads more men to hide that part away and express it privately.

Another thing that I think further widens the gap between how many men and women there are is the tendency in male sexuality to compartmentalize. That is, it seems like men are more willing to declare their sexuality based on a single thing (especially in the fetish community), while women are more likely to be less specific and tend towards ambiguity. Like how it seems like women are more likely to have a wider range of activities of interest to achieve the same level of sexual fulfillment, or how more men seem to hone in on specific things in order to be fulfilled."

*   *   *

She makes some great points. It does seem that groups geared more towards "age-play" garner more women than those geared towards diapers. Many men are attracted to the age-play aspects because of the diapers, while a greater portion of the women are attracted to the diapers because of the age-play. Of course, this is not true across the board. I should also mention that much of this is conjecture based on my (and her) experience. The sad reality is that there has never been much study on Infantilism. No group, online or in real life, could present the entirety of ABDLs without a major margin of error. Some online communities still command a 100:1 male domination, while other online and real life communities tend to have a more even split, like 5:4, or 1:1, and sometimes even 4:5 in favor of the ladies!

I've wracked my brain, and could not think of a study to conduct that would accurately depict everyone with ABDL interests in a fair manner. This is partially due to the unspecific definition of Adult Baby. What would be the requirements to be counted? An interest in diapers? An interest in playing baby? Actively wearing diapers and playing baby? All of the above? Any of the above? Change the requirements, and change the outcome.

Who would we ask? People on the street? An anonymous online gallery? Any online ABDL community would exclude those interested in the lifestyle, but not interested in talking about it online. As far as I can see, an accurate depiction is impossible. All I can do is guess based on my experience, and present it exactly as I have.

I insist that an accurate depiction is not necessary. It seems to me that by attempting this, we are after a label to classify a person as an "Adult Baby", and enjoy our preconceived notions of him. This is missing the point of seeing the unique individuality each person shows. No person can be truly understood with any collection of labels.

PEDOPHILIA?

The worst assumption you could make about an Adult Baby is that he is a pedophile. I can see how this relation is made. I like diapers, kids wear diapers, therefore I must like kids. Not so. I can't explain my drive to wear diapers, but I am certain there is no relation to children. I feel bad for anyone that is accused of being something so horrific because they are different and misunderstood. We like diapers. We do not like kids. Those that like Adult Babies like *adults* in diapers. They don't like kids.

Now, I'd love to say that there's not a single ABDL in the world that is attracted to children, but this can't possibly be the case. Prior to the 70s, when homosexuals were misunderstood, they, too, were accused of being pedophiles. Yet, today, can we confidently say that no homosexuals are pedophiles? Of course not. There must be pedophiliac ABDLs and homosexuals. We're all different people with different mixtures, so it's a numbers thing. Certainly, no assumptions should be made.

There is no link between ABDLs and pedophilia. To make this assumption is nothing short of discrimination.

IS IT A FETISH?

I don't like the term fetish. I feel that it carries with it a negative connotation. You hear "fetish" and you think "freak" or "mentally ill". There seems to be a fine line between fetish and, say, nibbling on the ear, or kissing on the neck. Kink is a better term. Kink suggests a difference in the fabric, which is much more accurate, as we all have them, and wearing diapers is no different than other "kinks".

Fetish demands sexual connotation as well, and as we have already learned, this is not always the case. That friend I mentioned who refuses all sexual aspects during his baby time can hardly be labeled as a fetishist. Kink could refer to sexual things and non-sexual things. That I eat my cereal with water instead of milk is a kink. I don't, but wouldn't that be so freaky?

Yes, even the term kink suggests sexuality, but that's more of a cultural standard than a true definition. The term referring to unconventional sexual preferences is slang. While the literal definition is fabric or rope related. I prefer the metaphor as it relates to people. To limit diapers to a fetish is to deny all asexual comfort so many people receive from them.

*   *   *

So, let's sum this up. What is an Adult Baby? I don't know. The best I can answer is that it is the blanket term to describe all people with any interest of any of the following things: diapers, wearing baby clothes, using baby items like bottles, pacifiers, or sippy cups, or role playing as a baby/toddler. This undefined nature of the term, "Adult Baby," used to describe us is likely the cause of all the misunderstanding about us.

Yet, this problem cannot be fixed with a more specific definition. The problem is not in the definition of the label, but the expectations and assumptions expressed upon the labeled.

LABELS

One learns I wear diapers, and labels me an Adult Baby. Once labeled an Adult Baby, assumptions are made: Mommy and Daddy didn't love me enough as a child; I'm incapable of having a healthy relationship; I'm a freak, or a pervert; I smell bad, or I love walking around in my own waste; or, at worst, I'm a pedophile.

Our society is addicted to labels. Labels help us understand things we see. They come in all shapes and sizes. You might find out someone is a salesman, and you would make presumptions based on that label. On a wider scale, you may look at a woman, and see that she's a woman, and make assumptions based on her gender as well. While this is a natural tendency, it is, to a point, self-defeating and potentially harmful to society.

So I get it. You learn I'm wearing a diaper, and it's so shocking and abnormal that our brains cling to any label it can gather to make sense of the situation, and "Adult Baby" is the closest thing we find. Our label of "Adult Baby" represents baby talk, stewing in human waste, mental instability, and possibly pedophilia. This assumption, of course, is stemmed from our lack of understanding, and is meaningless, but this is human nature after all.

There is a significant link between labels and judgment. We naturally use labels to help understand those that are different. After all, different from us, or different from normal, is considered bad.

We have a tendency in this society to deny ourselves the right to be different. We shame ourselves for our kinks and do our best to fit into the "normal" society. This normalness is perpetuated by others that "pretend" to be normal. The more people that join this "normal" group, the stronger it becomes, making it harder for other different people to fit in, encouraging them to hide their kinks, thus perpetuating the false notion of "normal", and so on. In reality, many of the people that seem normal are not. I have a theory that nobody is normal. The best way to hide our own kinks is to judge others for their kinks, giving us the strongest image of "normal". One glance at a PostSecret book shows how many people are different, or not "normal".

Ironically, the part of ourselves that judges others for being different is the same part of ourselves that judges ourselves for being different. The only thing that truly binds us all is that we are all different, so why shun the different?

The majority of people in the world have kinks. What makes one kink, like getting your ear nibbled, normal, while another kink, like wearing diapers, freakish, is imaginary. What makes these different is a matter of perspective and judgment, which exists only in your mind. What we consider "normal" is what is common, while uncommon is abnormal. *Normal is a societal expression of averages.* Without people to provide labels, there is no normal or abnormal.

So what's the solution? The solution does not lie within the Adult Baby, nor the label itself, but one's reliance upon the label. Practice getting out of the habit of labeling. We are all individuals, each with a different set of traits. I am not an Adult Baby. I am me, I am Brian, and I happen to be an Adult Baby, but this does not define me. It is but one of many traits.

Other people wear diapers and are nothing like me. Other people are AB's and don't wear diapers, and are nothing like me. We all have different traits, and some of them tend to overlap. One trait does not infer another. Any one trait says nothing of a person's other traits.

I am Brian. I, like all of you, am a unique individual, deserving of love and respect. One of the many things that make me unique is that I am an Adult Baby.

I write this book not to represent the entire AB community. No one person could possibly do that because the community is made up of individuals. I write this book to portray the individuality that makes one particular Adult Baby, and should act as a reminder to look at each person, no matter the label, as an individual person, just like you and me.

*   *   *

Despite the ambiguity of the term Adult Baby, it is an established term that I will use for the remainder of the book. Consider it more an adjective than a person. For ease of communicating, I will use the term as a blanket term that it is. Anyone into diapers, toddler age-play, or babyhood will be referred to as an Adult Baby, or AB. I do not intend to offend anyone by doing so, only to make the point of this book clearer. In many ways, the terms are interchangeable, as I am referring to the *people* with the interests. You may see that in my past I was more of a DL than an AB.

Some may find it hypocritical to bash the use of labels in one section, and perpetuate said labels in the other sections. These folks would be missing the point of my argument against the *importance* of labels. The label does not matter as much as the spirit behind it. No matter one's label, the person himself ought to be the focus.

Section 2:
The Life of Brian

This is my autobiography as it pertains to diapers. There has been much more that I've experienced that does not revolve around diapers, but it would be irrelevant in this book. This story is from the perspective of an Adult Baby. I tell this story so people can get insight into who I am as a person and what it's like being an Adult Baby, to prevent other Adult Babies from making the same mistakes I did, and to give parents (or spouses, or other loved ones of Adult Babies) a better grip on how to handle such a situation without causing the damage inadvertently done to me. This story is followed by two more sections containing deeper explanations and more guidance into these subjects about how to handle the difficult situations therein.

FROM CHILDHOOD

The year was 1984. I was three years old, and I had just woken up in the morning, the sunlight splashed across my bedroom walls over my Kermit the Frog poster. I just had the most amazing, wonderful dream. It was a perfect representation of my fantasy, in which I was small enough to fit into baby diapers.

In the dream, there were a bunch of little monkeys in an empty wading pool in the living room, and all were in diapers. I was among them, the same size, and diapered as well. I'm not sure of the significance of the monkeys. But to this day, thirty years later, I still remember the emotional impact that dream had on me.

I lay in bed trying to fall back asleep so I could continue the dream. That was how I wanted my life to be. Diapered and cared for forever.

I seem to remember having a desire for diapers at that point in my life. The dream was a manifestation of my desires, rather than the root or cause of them.

Unremitting, this dream stayed with me. Every night for at least a couple years beyond that morning I went to sleep thinking about the dream so I could dream it again. The dream never came back. Praying did not help, yet I continued relentlessly begging God to bestow the dream upon me again.

My heart ached. It took over my psyche. The other kids were playing cops and robbers and playing on the swings, and while I joined them, all I could think about was being diapered again. That's not to say it took over my life, but it most certainly was always there on some level, even at such an early stage of development.

It was around the time of the dream that my brother and sister, twins, were born. Did this have something to do with forming these desires in me? We can attempt some psychoanalysis till our faces are blue. Recently, I've come to the conclusion that the *why* of things matter far less than accepting the state of things. However, one could easily conjecture that with new children in the family, I felt like I was being replaced, and associated growing out of diapers with growing out of the top spot for my parents' attention. To seriously examine this conjecture, we'd have to ask why every person with a sibling three years younger doesn't crave diapers the way I do.

It's truly fascinating how so many people can experience the same thing and react in their own unique way. I'd read a study on cloned cows, and when a group of these identical cows with the exact same DNA were placed in a common pen, they developed their own hierarchy and individual personalities. Some of them became submissive, others became leaders, others aggressive, etc. What is it that makes these differences amongst us all if it's not DNA?

A quote from Robert Lanza, geneticist, in response to an attempt to clone a deceased pet:

> "Anyone who thinks they might be able to get Spot or Fluffy back is mistaken. Cloned animals have distinct personalities, just like identical twins. We cloned a herd of cattle several years ago -- they were all cloned from a single individual. Yet they developed a social-dominance hierarchy just like a herd of ordinary dairy cows. The cloned animals exhibit the full spectrum of behavioral traits, from curious and inquisitive to timid and shy. There's no doubt about it: each cloned animal has its own unique, individual personality." (See source in bibliography)

It is fascinating to consider that if we were to clone Hitler, he may be an artist. If we were to clone Einstein, he may be a plumber.

While being timid or inquisitive may be natural traits to have, a desire to wear diapers seems a little... off. I believe that a craving for diapers is as "natural" as timidity, just far more rare. What society considers normal is not more "natural" than the weird stuff, just more common. According to society, normal can simply be defined as "common." What is natural is how nature reacts to any given situation, and, as you can see, nature is made up of individual beings that each react differently.

After the dream, and after the twins were born, I rejoiced that there were diapers in the house once again. I'd sneak into the babies' room and grab a diaper or two, stow them out under my shirt into my room. They didn't really fit right, but it was exciting all the same. I loved everything about them. The plastic was smooth, the prints were cute, the perfume smelled amazing. They were so soft. I felt like I was breaking the rules, but I didn't even care. The drive towards diapers was far more intense than my drive to follow the rules and avoid punishment.

I tried to wear them, even though they didn't fit right. I would tear the sides in attempt to get them to reach the tapes, or I would experiment with taping two or three diapers together to see if I could recreate the diapered experience. What I found worked best was taping the diaper directly to my skin and keeping the diaper wrapped between my legs with underwear. It caused some really bad rashes where the tape was directly on my skin, but it didn't stop me. I loved it and wanted to be in diapers forever. I wanted so badly to have diapers that still fit me. I can't explain how much I desired this. Until I could acquire a fitting diaper and live in them full time, my life was incomplete. This was my state of mind.

For some reason, telling my parents was out of the question. I don't have adequate recollection from such a young age. Three year olds don't really have that sense of secrecy and individuality yet, so I don't see why I wouldn't have told my parents. One time I was told to clean my room, so I just shoved everything under the bed. Upon calling my father in to inspect my cleaning job, he responded with a "job well done", and I, in turn, bragged about my accomplishment by encouraging him to look under the bed. Clearly, I did not have a sense of what they would approve of and what they would not.

Without that natural sense, I make the educated guess that I *did* attempt to tell them I wanted to wear diapers, and was told that it was out of the question, I was too big for diapers, or I wasn't a baby anymore. This built in me a struggle between wanting approval from my parents, which every young child craves, and wanting to wear diapers, which I couldn't shake for the life of me.

I was four or five years old when my friend Riley was playing in my back yard with me while my mom did some gardening. I wanted to show Riley that I was wearing a diaper, but I also remember being certain that my mother would disapprove, and I didn't want to be grounded or spanked! So I told Riley to follow me to the side of the house, and I lifted up my shirt and pulled out the waste of my jeans. Riley was amazed that I was wearing a diaper. "Don't tell mom, k?" I said, and we then continued playing whatever we were playing.

This is my second earliest diaper related memory, the monkey dream being first, and it carries with it much significance. Why would I want to show Riley? Even at that young age I wanted acceptance and understanding. I craved these things, and felt I lacked them. My parents wouldn't accept me, so maybe my friend Riley would. He did, but I don't recall the acceptance being fulfilling or significant. At that age, I imagine we mostly float through lives living in each individual moment. To be that wise again would be nice for all of us.

*   *   *

I remember the dream, and I remember showing Riley my diaper. Beyond that, I don't really remember much until my teenage years. I do remember that my obsession with diapers never ceased or weakened throughout that time. I remember that every time we were at the grocery store I became uncomfortable walking through the diaper isle. This discomfort stemmed from wanting to buy the diapers, but not having money or the ability to ask for them, combined with the paranoia of being discovered. I stared at every bag of Pampers and Huggies with yearning, but forced myself to look away to appear normal. My muscles would tighten and my heart would race. There was much conflict within me. This is unfortunate for such a young child.

Once the twins were out of diapers when I was around six, my mother began a home business, doing daycare out of our home. This was quite convenient for my passion as there proved to always be a healthy stock of diapers around.

I would sneak a diaper or two to my room, tape them to my skin and pull them through my legs, wearing tight underwear to keep them in place. I would pee in them, then take them off. I couldn't risk being seen throwing a used diaper away, so I often elected to chuck the used diapers into the crawl-space. Nobody ever went up there anyway, so my secret was safe forever! Or so was my logic at the time. I recall being nervous every time a parent was shuffling around in the back of the basement, fearing that they may find my stash of dirty diapers. My childhood was overflowing with paranoia. It was exhausting.

My dad ended up cleaning the crawlspace one day when I was around eleven. I'm sure they'd had their suspicions by then, but it was before they knew the extent of the problem (their word, not mine). There was a four-foot pile of dirty diapers from the crawlspace that had accumulated over the years. They did not confront me about it.

While I had access to diapers, I still lacked access to diapers that *fit*. I would pray my heart out; pray for hours on end for God to send me diapers. Then I'd search the storage room in the basement for adult sized diapers I expected God to magically place hidden in the back somewhere. This went on for years.

Since the diapers I got were too small for me, and the ones in the store so expensive, I'd experiment with other things to simulate the diaper experience. "Maybe I could poke holes in this grocery bag for my legs and pull them up. That would simulate the plastic cover of a diaper." I would consider. "And for the inner stuffing, perhaps I could use these napkins." Not surprisingly, it didn't work at all, nor did any of my other attempts at making homemade diapers.

The worst experiment was, at the time, one of the scariest moments of my life. Now it's sort of funny, but also sad that I had to go through that. I was searching the garage for things with which I could create a makeshift diaper. "Hmmm… what reminds me of a diaper? Oh, this looks like a diaper. It has a big, soft, thick padding, just like a diaper. And it has an outer lining. It is paper, not plastic, but it should do. Plus, it has a cute pink panther on it, which is reminiscent of the childish prints on disposable diapers." This seemed too perfect, so I cut a diaper shape out of the strip of fiberglass insulation, wrapped it around me and taped it together on the sides.

Anyone that has touched fiberglass before knows well the burning sensation that follows. What I did not know at the time is that fiberglass insulation has millions of "fibers" of "glass" that will get stuck in your pores, causing an intense burning sensation. I might as well have made a diaper out of sewing needles! Five minutes after taping onto me the makeshift diaper, I was sitting on the floor of the shower, hot water raining down on me. I was crying from the pain, and thought the burning sensation in my crotch would never go away. I couldn't tell my parents because then they'd know I was playing diapers again. So I prayed. I thought God was punishing me for my evil ways. Diapers were not allowed, as was made clear by my parents, and God knows I disobeyed, so the punishment came in the burning rash on my bum, genitals, and waistline. I apologized profusely to God, and promised him that I would never wear diapers again.

The pain only lasted an hour or two and began to fade, but it was a very scary moment in my life. It added to the guilt I already had for wearing diapers. The promise I made to God was broken in a matter of days. I made that unfulfilled promise a few times, and that piled on more guilt. While the fiberglass story does seem a bit humorous upon recollection, I would not wish this experience on anyone, as it was quite traumatic.

There were also times that I'd spend my allowance on diapers. I'd make five bucks a week mowing the lawn, and it would take me a couple weeks to save up enough for an $8 bag of Pampers at the 7-11. After my allowance was saved, I'd ride my bike the mile to the convenience store, and dance around nervously in the isle, pretending I was looking at something else, until I could finally gather the courage to take the bag to the counter and pay for it. "They're not for me," I would say.

The man looked at me funny. "Well, of course not. I didn't think they were for you." I look back and it is so blatantly obvious that nobody would ever consider that the diapers were for me. But at that age, I was so self-conscious. I felt so different. It was as if the entire world could see directly into my soul and see that I was a fake, a freak that wanted to wear diapers. The vulnerability was excruciating.

I would occasionally drop hints with my friends. I'd say "If you could wear diapers again, would you?" or "What if we just wore diapers all day." I hoped that one might respond with "that would be so awesome!" No one ever did. The responses I got were "why would we do that?" or "you'd stink all day" or "That's really weird."

This confirmed my belief that I was alone in this world, a true freak with nobody to understand me.

Throughout my childhood, I felt alone, isolated, bad, and freakish. It was clear that I was different, and different was bad. There was something wrong with me. I had extremely strong feelings for diapers that nobody else had, and I couldn't tell anyone about it. I didn't choose to be bad. Rather, I felt a compulsion to be good! I wanted to be good, to treat people well, to do the right thing. I had this programming within me that made me want to wear diapers. I wanted to be good, but was programmed to be bad. I couldn't help it. This was beyond my control. It was during this stage of development that my low self-esteem germinated as the guilt became overbearing.

THROUGH THE TEENS

It was in my early teenage years that things took a turn for the worse. My mom ceased her daycare business, so I no longer had my constant diaper supply. The only diapers I could get my hands on were the ones I would buy myself. It took me two weeks to save up enough money to buy a pack of Pampers that did not fit me. I could have saved up for four weeks and had enough to buy a pack of adult sized diapers that would actually fit me, but that would also entail four agonizing diaperless weeks. After two weeks, I'd get desperate and break down, scrambling to buy whatever I could get my hands on.

That didn't necessarily stop me from experimenting. I'd still ride my bike an extra few miles to get to the Safeway for some adult products. While the adult diapers themselves were entirely too expensive, some other adult products were a bit more affordable and under the two-weeks' worth of allowance mark. These products included pads, undergarments, and anything else that I thought could work as a diaper. I was never satisfied with any of them, though. I needed real diapers; plastic backing, tapes around the sides; diapers.

I was still as desperate for diapers as ever, and as I entered puberty more confused, unconfident and awkward as ever, my parents were becoming much more vocal about their disapproval of diapers. There was no understanding. Venturing into my teenage years, what I needed was acceptance and guidance. I was confused. I didn't know why I wanted to wear diapers, and I knew it wasn't normal, but what do I do? That's not to mention the normal teenage confusion about how to talk to girls, make friends, and the like. Rather than helping me, my parents gave me orders. Yet, orders against nature cannot be followed. The desire to wear diapers remained stronger than my desire to obey my parents. They expected me to be someone that I was not.

Early on, they discouraged me from wearing diapers, telling me I could never have a normal life in diapers. No woman would ever want to date me; ergo nobody would ever love me if I continued to wear diapers. Their logic was to present diapers in such a way that not wearing them was the obvious choice. That was based on the presumption that I was able to quit, or that it was a choice. Since it was not so simple, they inadvertently were just tearing me down. I was told that something was wrong with me mentally, and I really needed some psychiatric help. What I heard through my fifteen year old ears was "you're insane!" Harsh enough, yes, but it got worse.

The first time I bought a diaper that actually fit me was invigorating, and I remember it vividly to this day. I had worked it out like a heist. Cue the Mission Impossible theme. I was fifteen. My family was at the mall doing some Christmas shopping in early December. I'd had the right to shop alone and keep what I bought hidden under the guise that I was buying gifts for them. Bwahahaha! There was a Walgreens at this mall, and at Walgreens in the mid-nineties, they sold a six-pack of adult diapers for $5.99. Rather than risk carrying them around my parents, I remember hiding them under the seat of the car, and I made sure to sit on the side of the backseat on the way home as the seat was higher up. We arrived home, and everyone went to their respective rooms. A few hours later, I grabbed the keys, climbed out my window, grabbed all the diapers from under the car seat, and snuck them back into my bedroom window, with no one the wiser! I tried it on in my room as the Monorail episode of The Simpsons played. It was... a relief. It was something I'd sought after and dreamt of for over ten years, and finally, it had happened. The fantasy in the monkey dream twelve years before had finally become a reality. My entire life I wanted to be diapered again, and finally, I was.

*   *   *

I learned around this time that my mother had a drinking problem that had lasted for years. Looking back, it's obvious, but at the time, I had nothing to compare it to, so it appeared normal. But it was around this time that she began her recovery process. As she sobered up, the days of getting away with wearing diapers were coming to a close. The suspicion arose when she stopped daycare, but months later continued to find diapers around the house. There came a point where she could no longer brush off the diapers she found as part of her drunken stupor. My infatuation had been obvious enough in the past, yet easy enough to brush off. Find a diaper in the basement? She must have absentmindedly left it down there after changing one of the babies. Alcohol makes you do far dumber things than that. Now, though, there is no alcoholism to blame, and no babies around. Something was amiss. So began the most difficult time of my youth.

My parents asked if I was having bladder control problems, but I was proud, and I said "no way!" For some reason I felt like if I had admitted to having a bladder control problem, I would be so embarrassed! *Wanting* to wear diapers was embarrassing, too, but at least it was the truth. I'm not sure why, but I couldn't say yes to this question. Of course, that would have been the best option for me. I say yes, and they not only allow me to wear diapers thinking it is a medical issue, they would buy them for me! They probably would have been happier in the bliss of not thinking they raised a freak. I wished for years and years that I had said yes. Even to this day, I firmly believe that had I lied and said yes, my life would have taken a much better course than it did.

My parents would sit me down and explain to me the importance of not wearing diapers. They would explain to me that it's wrong, and that God disapproves and so do they. I wanted to be good and loved, so I would swear off diapers for good. But I could never last more than about three or four months before the drive overpowered me, and I'd find myself sneaking out again to buy more diapers, feeling guiltier than ever that I'm letting down my family, myself, and God. I tried as hard as I possibly could, and it wasn't good enough. I tried with all my heart, and I never could quit diapers.

When I was around sixteen, I was old enough to drive, and I had a job that provided a steady stream of income, much of which went to adult diapers. Sometimes I would dare myself to wear a diaper to school. I did, a few times. It was comforting, exciting, nerve-wracking, and guilt-ridden. On the one hand, this is how I wanted my life to be, diapered 24/7. If I could only get the school nurse to change me, it'd be perfect. On the other hand, I was terrified that everyone could tell, or that I might get caught. Each time I indulged in wearing a diaper to school, I'd always excuse myself to the restroom after an hour or two to remove it.

The greatest thing I lacked in my life was acceptance. I had none, and didn't know how to accept myself without others accepting me. On the surface, I was nice enough, social enough, but knowing on the inside that I was not who I was portraying made me very uncomfortable and unconfident in day to day life. Because of this lack of confidence, I had trouble making friends. The few friends that I did have were friends with the portrayal of me, and not the true me, whom I was certain could not possibly maintain any friendships. My parents seemed to hate me for the diaper wearing aberration I turned out to be. I had nobody to accept me for who I was. Later in life, I'd learn the importance of self-acceptance, but this was never taught to me in my teens. It's difficult to love and accept yourself when nobody else loves or accepts you.

One thing helped. It was around age fifteen that we got this incredible new thing in our home: the internet. Back in 1996, it was a big deal. After the five minutes of anti-melodic tones coming from the back of the computer, I was free to search webpage after webpage, with as little as fifteen minutes of loading time between each. Early on, I explored chat rooms and joke sites and typical teen age stuff. But one day, I had a genius idea to search adult diapers. I couldn't possibly recall the site itself. It wasn't really a webpage; it was more like a forum. The post went something like this:

"I really enjoy seeing adult women in diapers, and I like to wear them myself. Does anyone know where I can find other like-minded adults?"

The clouds parted, and the angels sang down on me. I WAS NOT ALONE! There was this one guy, probably a million miles away, with no description whatsoever, who was also into diapers! I was not the only freak of nature on the planet! It is impossible to explain the wave of emotions that came over me. Excitement, relief, amelioration, comfort, belonging, validation. It's so hard to describe. I'd lived my entire life believing that the world in its entirety was one way, and I alone was different. That day, though, I found one other person that was like me. If you've never felt so out of place, you couldn't possibly relate.

This discovery inspired me. Upon more searching, I found entire groups of people into diapers the same way I was! Not only that, but they were active members of society! They kept their diaper interests hidden, but were still able to live their lives. They worked, had relationships, friends, and even spouses. It was the community I had yearned for my entire life, but it did not last long. Once my parents found these diaper related sites on the search history, my computer privileges, along with that community that gave me a sense of belonging I had never experienced before, were stripped from me.

*   *   *

One time I did something exceptionally stupid. Let me rephrase that. I've done many exceptionally stupid things, and here is one! I found a diaper delivery service in the phone book. They agreed to deliver a case of adult diapers (a case usually consists of a box of around 60-100 diapers) to me the following day. My parents would be out until around five, but they could have shown up any time. To be extra safe, I gave them the address to a neighbor who was a family friend of sorts. They said they would deliver around three o'clock, so I went over there at one and sat on the curb in front of their house. Just hanging out. Sitting, waiting, anticipating. Hours later, they had still not arrived! I am getting nervous. The neighbors will be home soon, and my parents, too, and they cannot be delivered if they are in the vicinity. Five o'clock came and went. Everyone was home, and I had to make some cheesy excuse to hang out outside the neighbor's house all night, both to my parents and the neighbor. It was around half-past seven when I finally gave up. They must not be coming. I was disappointed, and felt like an idiot for standing out there all day for nothing, embarrassing myself in front of the neighbors. I went home and relaxed the night away. Until, that is, around 9:30 pm when the phone rang. It was the neighbors saying that some guy was delivering adult diapers to Brian! My parents looked at me, and I played dumb. "What? That's crazy? How weird is that? I certainly didn't order them! That'd be ridiculous!" Like they didn't know exactly what was going on. "I better go check it out," I said.

I ran over there, and insisted through the confusion that there was some sort of mistake. Obviously, what had happened was some other kid was playing a prank on me, and saw me enter your home once before as a guest, and assumed that this was my address. Yes, that's the only explanation that makes sense at all. The delivery guy seemed defeated, but left. I ran up the street, and waited for him to drive by and waved him down. I apologized for the fiasco and paid him cash, and he gave me the case. I hid the case outside somewhere so I could return home empty-handed and perform my exceptional acting skills for my family. "How crazy was that, huh? It must have been some sort of prank." I snuck them into my room through the bedroom window later that night when everyone else was asleep. It was a humiliating and stressful experience, but in the end I got my diapers. $65 well spent, all in all.

"What an idiot!" you're thinking. Looking back, that's what I'm thinking. I also recall the frustration during that period in my life. Desperate times call for desperate measures. "Desperate" is definitely the word to describe that time in my life.

*   *   *

With each diaper my parents continued to find around the house, the more their frustration grew, and the anger increased. That $65 case of diapers I'd worked so hard for was gone in a day or two. Not because I went through them all. On the contrary, I cherished the diapers. They were decent quality, fit me well, and having a good supply hidden in the back of my closet under a blanket was what I'd always wanted. It was only two days later that I came home from school with the mother's typical "we need to talk" stance. Oh, how I hated those words. "We need to talk" boiled up all the guilt I carried with me every day. And what did I have to feel guilty about? Wearing diapers, and lying to my parents. The diapers I couldn't help, and the lying I had no choice, but the guilt was heavy nonetheless. She had found my stash. Since she couldn't possibly allow her teenage son to indulge in diapers as they would most certainly ruin his life, she and my dad agreed that the best thing to do was to donate the diapers. $65 out the window, the case I worked so hard to get, enduring so much humiliation, gone forever. That they were gone hurt more than being caught. Wearing diapers never caused any pain in my life. It was the lack of acceptance that ruined my life.

This began a vicious cycle. I'd spend the money I made working at a hotel on adult diapers. My parents would periodically raid my room, searching the closet, under the bed, etc., looking for my stash and throwing them out. I had no privacy, no respect, no acceptance, and no dignity. They yelled at me a lot, to the point of being verbally abusive. "I couldn't be more disappointed in you, if you were gay" was the most hurtful one. "Nobody could ever love you" was the most damaging one.

They accused me of being a child molester. This is a common connection people make. If one has some sexual attraction to diapers, and children wear diapers, then one must have sexual attraction to children. Not the case. In fact, I did feel a little funny, perhaps a little awkward around kids in diapers. There was some odd sense of sexual arousal. I feared my parents were right; that I *was* a child molester. I avoided being around children from then on.

My parents had no shortage of ammunition for insisting I was insane, and that I needed help. I believed them, so I eventually asked for the psychiatric help they'd suggested years prior.

I started seeing this Christian psychiatrist who promised to help me through my recovery with a regimen of prayer. If nothing else, it gave my parents hope that maybe I would "heal" and become normal, so it got them off my back for a while. They paid $110 a week for me to go see him. The first visit he and I talked about diapers. The next week, though, he didn't bring it up. He didn't ask me about diapers. I think he asked how my week went, and I told him about how stressed I was at home and at school. Diapers never came up. The third week, he asked how I was doing, and again, I told him about home life and school. This continued for months. My parents were paying big money to cure me of my diaper fetish, and diapers never came up. I am sure it was part of his therapy regimen to wait for the patient to bring it up.

I had been seeing my therapist for about eight months when he told my parents that I never wanted to talk about diapers. My parents lost it, and a screaming match ensued. The fact is I *did* want to talk about diapers. My parents had no right to be mad. They spent my entire life covering my obsession with diapers with a blanket of shame, and then expect me to talk openly about it? Come on! I was ashamed! It was an unfair expectation placed on me at the time.

I never really felt like I was being "cured". During the times I spent refraining from diapers, my desires were no less than before. I just "pretended" that I was normal, because I so wanted to be. My parents encouraged this "pretending". They wanted me to really be normal, but I was not. It's not like there's a button I can push and instantly find the idea of wearing diapers preposterous.

I wanted to be in diapers 24/7. This was a fact. They wanted me to be normal. This was an unrealistic desire. They made me want to be normal. This was an unrealistic desire put upon myself. I wanted to make them proud, but this, too, was unrealistic, as a normal lifestyle was necessary for them to be proud of me. So, we all pretended. We didn't talk about it, as we were all ashamed of me. Why they expected me to talk openly about it after years of being trained not to is beyond me.

Now that I'm thirty-three, and I can look back at this situation and see clearly the nuances of why I did what I did. At the time, though, I was a confused sixteen year old. I went to see the psychiatrist, and I wanted him to make me normal, but I didn't realize that I had to bring it up. Nobody told me. At the very least, it should have been explained to me by the psychiatrist. My parents were royally pissed that I was "wasting" their hard earned money on professional help when I wouldn't even do my part. How did I feel about that at age sixteen? Guilty. I was such a mess, I couldn't even receive therapy properly! I just wanted to be normal.

I keep saying that the guilt was heavy, but this doesn't fully convey my feelings. With each time I tried to quit and failed, each time my parents yelled at me and expressed their disappointment, each time I wore a diaper knowing it was wrong, I hated myself a little more. I really, truly hated myself. I avoided looking at myself in the mirror. I felt unworthy to exist. I had such deep self-anger, resentment, and pure hatred, it is no wonder that I lagged behind in my social life.

After the blow up regarding my lack of effort in therapy, I went back to the therapist, and I was angry with him. I asked him why he didn't bring up diapers ever before when he knew I needed the help. He responded by asking me why I hadn't brought up diapers. I had no answer. At sixteen, I lacked the self-awareness and communication skills. So we talked about diapers that day, and I felt good about it. The next week I returned, but again, diapers didn't come up, as was the case each following visit thereafter. A few months later, my parents gave up on therapy and stopped paying for it. I was upset because I felt like that was my only hope to become normal. I felt like they were giving up hope, as there were no future plans. The therapy wasn't helping, and in that sense it was a waste of money. That guy was a joke. Even still, I harbor some resentment towards him. He's a paid professional that couldn't see the obvious situation that I was silent on the subject because I was ashamed of myself, thanks to the environment provided by my parents. I can see it clearly now, and I'm no trained therapist.

They were right to take me out of therapy, but for the wrong reasons. My parents were hoping for a normal child. Giving up hope was the right move because they were hoping for something imaginary. First, normal is make-believe. It's an expression of averages. It's based on opinions, not facts. Second, they were trying to change a part of me that had far deeper roots than they were aware.

One positive thing that came from the visits to the psychiatrist was that I could get away from my parents long enough to stop by the medical supply stores and shop for diapers. It is a bit ironic that I would stop by to indulge in the very thing I was on my way to cure. Don't doubt that I felt guilty over that, too. The trips to buy diapers were what I truly looked forward to, though. One particular medical supply store was called the "Get Well Store", with a particularly nice selection of adult diapers. I know it was awkward for a sixteen year old walking in claiming to be incontinent and asking about the different brands. It was the naughty, guilty feeling you get when you know you're doing something wrong. My mom found a piece of paper in my room that had written on it "The Get Well Store" and a phone number. She accused me of visiting a prostitute. Such was her opinion of my lifestyle. I denied, but I couldn't tell her the truth, as that would not have given her any solace, nor would it have made it easier on me.

*   *   *

Right around the time I started therapy, I got my first girlfriend. Sixteen felt really late to start dating. Most of my friends had had all sorts of relationships up until then. I was relieved to finally have a sense of belonging. I confessed to her after a month or two that I liked diapers. I was so scared, but she was totally cool about it! It was a big moment in my life in which I learned that my parents were wrong, that I *was* loveable. People *could* accept me. My sixteenth year held some positive growth for me, but no part of that growth was due to my therapist. I just began to realize that my parents didn't know everything about me.

The relationship didn't last more than a year, but the feeling that I was capable of being loved was very helpful to me. Far down the road, I would learn that love and acceptance from others could never possibly take the place of loving and accepting myself. Still, my life did seem to get a little better. With my first girlfriend came my first taste of acceptance.

As I traversed my late teens, the frustration level rose. My parents were fighting with each other more and more often, and more fiercely. They would go to couple's counseling, which I appreciated, and came back fighting even worse, which I despised. I was getting older and desired assertion of my independence more each day. I was becoming an adult, and quickly realizing that I did not belong under my parents' roof.

*   *   *

My desperation for acceptance manifested in strange ways. There was a part of me that was suppressed, hidden by force, which was dying to crawl its way out. It wanted to be seen, heard, loved, and accepted. I would find myself daring myself to do crazy things to be seen. I would strip down to a diaper and, say, run around the school in the middle of the night. What a rush! It felt like freedom, in a way. I couldn't explain why I needed to do those things at the time, but I now feel like it was to mimic certain needs that had yet been unfulfilled. The bigger the chance of being seen, or getting caught, the more satisfying it became. Then, every time I didn't get caught, it was a bit of a letdown.

This came to a crescendo at eighteen. I had just gotten off work at midnight. I drove to the back of a gigantic multiplex movie theater and stripped down to a diaper. I used it in the car, enjoying the diaper soaking up the wetness. These feelings remained every bit as pleasurable as they had been when I was three years old. I changed into a fresh diaper.

Here's the dare. I would take this dirty diaper, I'd walk it up to the dumpster, throw it away, and walk back to the car. Wearing only shoes and a diaper, I accepted this dare. It was such a rush! The crisp wind hit my exposed skin, exasperating the nerves. At any moment, someone could exit out of any one of the back exit doors of the theater, and there I would be, wearing only a diaper, like a baby. I was not after humiliation, but exposure. It was as if I just needed to verify that I existed. I had made it to the dumpster, and tossed in the wet diaper, wrapped into itself like a ball. Made it! Now, to get back. I was playing with fire, and I knew it. The guilt suddenly got the better of me, and I ran back to the car. Nobody had seen me. I'd gotten away with it! So exciting! So exhilarating! So…. Unsatisfying. Why was I unsatisfied? Maybe it was because the challenge hadn't been extreme enough.

So, I went back out. I ventured out to the front of the building, the main traffic area of the complex. It was late. There were a few stragglers still leaving. I snuck around. Still, I was wearing only a diaper and tennis shoes. Still chilly. The breeze just added to the excitement. I'd made it to the edge of the parking lot. There was a grassy median and a brick wall I ducked behind. Peeking over, planning my next move, one guy spotted me. He was so far away, probably 150 yards, walking out of the main entrance with some friends. He pointed at me, and I ducked back down. My mind buzzed! CAUGHT! This is not what I wanted! "Oh shit oh shit oh shit, what am I going to do? Please just keep walking." I looked again. He was running right towards me! I couldn't run away or I'd be completely exposed. At least now my nearly naked and diapered body was hidden behind a wall. I peed. The warmth felt nice. I did not know what to do. He was approaching fast, and I lifted my head up when he was about twenty feet away. He stopped from a sprint with a hint of panic.

"Dude, are you ok?" the 20-something guy asked me.

"Yes, totally good." I started forming this story in my mind that it was a high school prank, or a hazing ritual or something, but he didn't push the subject. He really was just concerned for me, so he left. He probably thought I was a lost mentally challenged kid. God, the guilt was unbearable. I had to get back. I ran back to the car. On the way back, I neared a ridge, and a family was walking below. I juked left and got out of their sight as quickly as possible, but they saw me. I'm sure they did. I made it back to my car. Safety. Relief.

Yet… still, I craved more.

Why? To this day, I can't explain it. A part of it was that I was a teen in rebellion. Teenagers rebel. It's a known fact. Sure, most kids drag race and try alcohol, the forbidden nectar. But for me, diapers were the forbidden nectar that I craved - diapers, and acceptance for being diapered. Being caught running around in only a diaper seems like a ridiculous way to achieve acceptance. I was lost, desperate, unguided, and our minds do crazy things sometimes.

The craving continued. I should have driven away immediately, but I did not. I sat in my car and examined what I'd done. Was I being crazy? Yes. Was I willing to end up in jail for this? Hell no! Why, then, do I want more? It was like a little addiction of its own. Maybe I just wanted the adrenaline, but I had one final dare. It was late enough now that the complex was essentially deserted. My diaper was wet, and I needed a change. I'd already successfully thrown the last one away, so the odds of success in throwing this one away was a lock! After the close calls I just had, this feels pretty tame.

I changed in the car, and I walked to the dumpster carrying the balled up wet diaper, wearing only tennis shoes and a fresh diaper. The diaper goes in the trash, and a leisurely diapered stroll back to the car will end the night. What I did not anticipate, however, was the security guard doing his final grounds walk of the night. He turned the corner and stared at me. I stopped, turned, and bolted! "STOP! GET BACK HERE!" he barked with attempted authority. I was literally afraid of being shot! But I didn't stop. I looked over my shoulder. He was chasing me, but he was overweight, and I was fast. I took a breath of relief as I sprinted away, widening the gap. I would have to run all the way around the building to get back to my car now! I checked back again to gauge his relative speed, but he was no longer running. Rather, he was calmly walking, and talking into his radio. Two plus two.... He's calling his partner to cut me off! If I can't go around, I'll go out. Took a ninety-degree turn and ran straight through the parking lot. The security guard was no longer calm! He was barking and running again. This gave me some hope that I'd made the right decision.

I sprinted the length of the lot, then through about a hundred yards of a large weedy field in which my shoe nearly fell off before I turned a corner of an office building to look back. He was just now waddling into the weeds! I had plenty of time to tie my shoe and pray to God to let me out of this one. Shoe tied. Now I had options. Continue to run away, or take another ninety-degree turn. I was behind a building now, so either way, he wouldn't know my direction. I chose the turn. Still sprinting through the field, I backtracked. He wouldn't expect it, and I'd stay close to my car. I passed a couple more buildings and approached a bank. I found a good place to hide behind a dumpster and a fence. They would be unable to find me without climbing over one of them. And there I squatted, wearing only a diaper and tennis shoes, in the December cold. I was scared. I had recently turned eighteen, officially legal, so I could easily go to jail for this one. I assumed I was breaking one law or another. On the bright side, the police would not have to tell my parents. I sat and I prayed. I prayed that they wouldn't find me. Yet again, I promised God that I would never wear a diaper again if he got me out of this one. This one wasn't an empty promise. I promised him repeatedly for five minutes, ten minutes, fifteen minutes.

It must have been twenty minutes before I decided to assess the situation. Maybe they'd given up the hunt by now. As quietly as possible, I climbed over the dumpster, edged my way down the brick wall, and poked an eye beyond to see whatever I could see. The weeds danced in waves with each gust, and a searchlight swept the field from the other side of the bank. Red and blue lights were lighting up alternating parts of the field. Not only were they still looking, the police were called in as well. So I returned to my spot and continued to pray. I prayed they would not bring the canine units in. And I cried. What had I gotten myself into? My parents were right! I'm worthless. A criminal! Maybe I belong in jail. The thought of turning myself in did not cross my mind. My self-preservation engine was full throttle. The guilt and self-hatred were unyielding. Another five minutes passed. Ten. It was getting colder, but I was literally trapped. Fifteen.

Twenty more minutes had passed since I saw the search light, and it was time to reassess my position. I stood and lifted one leg onto the dumpster, and heard a police siren very close. Just for a second. Did he see me? Have I been found? I dropped back down to my spot immediately. Waiting... Waiting... Nothing. After a minute, I started breathing again. Still, it was too soon to leave. I'd been hiding behind this dumpster in the cold, wearing only a diaper, wallowing in my self-pity and disgust for forty minutes now, and the cops were right outside. What was I to do? Five more minutes. Praying. Ten more minutes. I stole another glance outside over the fence. Red and blue lights still splashed on the field. It was on the other side of the field now, but it would be incredibly too risky to make a break for it now. More waiting was in order. I punished myself emotionally.

I swore off diapers for good. This was ridiculous. I'm a terrible person. The police are after me! I probably belong in jail! I sat in that nook made up of a bank, a wooden fence, and a dumpster, for an hour and fifteen minutes before I was able to escape safely. I scanned the field. No people, no lights. I edged around, scanned the parking lot. No movement. There were only about twenty cars scattered throughout the vast asphalt. I stared, watched the lot for a few minutes. I checked each car individually. Nothing. Now or never. I sprinted back to my car, dove in, and drove off.

The relief was great, but so was the feeling that I'd gotten away with something. Yet, even on the way home I accepted another self-dare, stopping by a small strip mall and taking another diapered run.

I came home hours late. My mom was sleeping on the couch. They'd been fighting again. She asked me where I was, and I said I was at work. I did not attempt to explain the two hour time discrepancy. She accused me of lying. I denied. It was probably too late to fight about it, so that was the end.

*   *   *

My parents ended up divorcing. I did not approve of this. They'd told me from a young age that marriage was permanent. They were setting a poor example. No. It was worse than that. They were being hypocrites. My mom moved out and got her own apartment a few miles away. I had the ability to choose who to go with, and I chose to stay at home. The choice was not a preference of one parent over the other. My feelings towards each were extremely hostile. They were both incredibly mean. Neither of them loved me. I just wanted to stay at home, and felt like staying home was some form of stand against the divorce.

My dad worked a lot, so that was nice. I had the house to myself most of the time, which was a positive. As I had gotten older, I naturally acquired more freedom. I was able to visit these diaper websites from school, friends' houses (when they weren't watching), or even my own house, when my dad wasn't around. I no longer had constant supervision, so I was able to shop for whatever diapers I wanted whenever I wanted. Things weren't all perfect, though.

I was not doing well in school. Considering the emotional state I was in, I'm not surprised. I struggled socially. The raids continued. I had a friend over one time when my dad lost his temper and screamed and yelled at me for an hour. My dad was not subtle, either. He mentioned diapers numerous times. "You're an eighteen year old in DIAPERS!" he yelled once, right in front of my friend, as if I was just the most ridiculous thing in existence, and so obviously did not belong in this world. Thank God that particular friend already knew that I wore diapers. I had met him through a diaper site and we became friends. It was after about forty minutes of me standing there in front of the window idly while my father screamed in my face that my friend realized this wasn't going to end any time soon and he left. I hated my dad for doing that. Resorting to humiliating me in front of my friends is not punishment, it is abuse.

I did get to meet a few people from my online communities. I never really clicked with anyone in particular. They were nice enough people. It turns out it is difficult to form a friendship over one specific interest. That did not stop me from searching for love through these sites. One out of fifty of these members was the sought after female Adult Baby! It took a few years to realize that an interest in diapers is not enough to form a relationship over, either. I know it should have been obvious, but the idea of getting romantic interests to accept this diapered part of me was extremely intimidating. Seeking girls already into diapers seemed much easier. Easier is not better, so I've since learned, but this is a lesson that took some time to figure out.

It was unfortunate that my friends that were into diapers, I felt, lacked a certain chemistry that is so essential in any lasting friendship. My day to day friends, however, I was unwilling to tell that I enjoyed diapers for fear of rejection. What I had was no true friends, and many pseudo-friends. This was not the fault of the friends, of course. This was my own fault for not being my true self. But by now it should be obvious why that was not the most appealing course of action either.

*   *   *

I don't recall how it happened, but I found myself on the telephone with my mom while I was at work. She mentioned that a few months ago, that night I came home very late from work, she knew what I was up to because she saw the story on the news with the theater. I still acted like I didn't know what she was talking about. In my head I thought, *That made the news?!* The conversation was not pleasant. She was telling me that she loved me, and I was telling her that I didn't believe her, and that I did not love her. It was not resolved that night, but I did feel very down on myself about it. A good person would love his mother. I did not, therefore - you get the idea. Come to think of it, I never did believe her, or my dad, when they told me that they loved me. They'd tell me they loved me, and they'd tell me often. Their actions told a different story. I do not remember feeling love growing up. I felt unloved and unlovable. Feeling unlovable certainly contributes to feeling unloved. They'd tear me apart one day and tell me how worthless I was, and express their love for me the next. The claims appeared hollow. I believed they were telling me they loved me because that's what was expected of them as parents, but I knew the truth. Today, as a matured (relatively) adult, I still struggle to believe that they loved me. I think they did, in fact, believe they loved me, but lacked the wisdom to truly love.

INTO ADULTHOOD

I wanted to leave the current tense situation living with my dad. Back when I was twelve years old I wanted to move out on my own. It wasn't some silly childish rebellion. I really wanted to move out, and, given the chance, I would have. I needed to get out of that environment even back then. I knew it when I was twelve, and I knew it throughout my teen years until I was twenty. I'd graduated high school, barely. I was working in a hotel making not amazing money. I didn't know how to get a better job, and I could not afford my own apartment. The thought of getting a roommate wasn't entirely appealing because I'd still lack the freedom to wear diapers as I wanted. Even a roommate situation, though, would have been too expensive. The solution came when a high school friend called me about a year after graduating to tell me that he and a bunch of his college friends were getting a big house, and they needed people to fill rooms to make it affordable. The short of it was that I had the opportunity to move out, and it'd only cost me $225 a month! Very doable. I did not hesitate, and within a month, I was there.

I remember vividly lying in my bed in my new room that very first night. The window was open, and I could hear the train in the distance. Finally I had escaped. Finally, freedom. The day I moved out was the best day of my life, and remained so until age thirty. It felt like my first day of freedom after a lifetime in prison.

It was not ultimate freedom, mind you. Just better. I still had peers in the house. We all got along really well. Not so well that I could tell them I enjoyed diapers, but well. Even with my then ex-girlfriend's acceptance, I was nowhere near ready to put myself out there like that. I did not welcome such vulnerability.

My room was right off the main living room area. I could buy diapers from a medical supply store down the street a half mile or so, carry them back while most of my roommates were in college, and bring them in my bedroom window to avoid those roommates that might be home at the time. I'd hide them in the back of my closet or under the bed with relatively little suspicion. No random diaper raids here. One roommate said it smelled like I wet the bed once, but I brushed it off. At least I maintained a fair amount of privacy. No more raids. It really was nice. I became much more calm and content. The temper I'd had at home was gone. I realized what a terrible environment "home" really was only after I moved away to experience something so much better and more peaceful.

It was an uneventful year in that nothing of major significance happened. Moving out in itself was entirely significant, however, and I can't stress this enough. It was a transition from a dark, cloudy hell to beautiful, bright freedom. The transition was immediate the very day I moved out.

During the year in the new town, an hour and a half from my old home, my mom would visit occasionally. She started expressing deep regret for how I was treated growing up. I held resentment, but parental approval was all I ever wanted. At twenty, I was not too old for it. I was a little reluctant, but I appreciated the gestures. She explained that much of the tension was cross fire between her and my dad. I doubted that because she often yelled at me when my father was nowhere near, but I could tell that she was trying to repair the relationship, and I welcomed this. She did not treat me like a disappointment anymore. Through this year, we had some really great talks and, for the first time in my life, started forming a real relationship with my mother.

I saw my dad occasionally, too, but it was not the same. He expressed no regret. He would invite me over for dinner, we'd chat and be cordial, and that was all. The underlying problems remained. I felt like we were fine as long as we pretended that we didn't go through all the troubles before.

As my lease for that room expired, I figured that if I saw that great a jump in happiness from home to a roommate situation, I could expect a similar jump moving into my very own apartment. Unfortunately, I got suckered into a lease agreement that was far beyond my financial capabilities. Lesson learned. The amazing job I'd landed was proving to be not so amazing. I struggled to pay rent, but I still needed diapers. Desperately. If I didn't have diapers, I would get very depressed, anxious, and uneasy. I was not happy unless I had diapers. So, how did I get diapers with no money? Well, some would call it breaking and entering. Ocean's 11 was out, and I loved the idea of pulling off my own masterminded heist. I succeeded many times, stealing cases of adult diapers at a time, but I quickly realized that this was not the way I wanted my life to go. Stealing is bad. I knew that. The desperation just overpowered me. I have never stolen from a store in the past, nor ever since.

That's not entirely true. I did steal a bag of Pull-ups from my best friend's closet when we were thirteen. I am sure he did not need them any longer and they would eventually be thrown out, but I couldn't very well ask for them. In a way, I feel worse about the pull-ups, because I betrayed a good friend.

*   *   *

Living alone was nice. I could lounge around wearing only a diaper if I wanted. That type of freedom is what I had dreamt of all my life. My social life was getting more difficult, though. The bigger part of my life diapers became, the more awkward around others I felt. I did not feel like I could tell them I wore diapers. They'd brand me a freak. I certainly would not make any friends that way. By hiding it, though, I felt like nobody knew me. I was alone. Empty. People were friendly with my portrayal of me, but not the true me.

I did occasionally find some people I clicked with. I was waiting tables at a restaurant one night and got along very well with a table of three, who eventually invited me to sit. We all became pretty good friends, and one girl, Kayleigh, became an interest. The attraction was mutual, and once I felt like it was safe, I opened up to her, told her that I enjoyed wearing diapers. She thought I was joking, and that hurt me, but it eventually worked out. I clicked with her like no other person before. She was definitely a part of my destiny. She and I ended up seeing each other, off and on, for ten years.

During the off periods, though, I developed a bad habit. The craving for acceptance never went away, and I thought back to the times I was accepted. I had my first girlfriend, and I had Kayleigh. My mind made the connection that women with whom I am romantically entangled provide acceptance. The habit that developed was that of me confessing to women that I wore diapers in attempt to get that acceptance. Some accepted me, and it boosted my confidence level, however temporary. Others rejected me, and I spiraled into self-loathing depression. Ups and downs, yet never truly happy. When down, I'd seek out any acceptance I could find, and this often came in the form of Kayleigh.

While my mom and I did have a relationship at the time, it did not provide the acceptance I needed. It was leaps and bounds better than my teenage years, but the subject of diapers was still off limits. It made her uncomfortable. She still did not know how to handle it. To her credit, she did learn to love me even though she didn't understand. Most definitely, it was a big step in the right direction.

To put it frankly, I used Kayleigh. I didn't know I was using her. I didn't set out to use her, or plan to. I was unknowingly using her for *my* needs. Even though I didn't know it at the time, I kept returning to her not because I was in love with her and couldn't stay away, but because I needed some form of acceptance, and she could provide that for me. She truly knew me better than anyone else, and she still loved me. I didn't even love myself. If I was to receive any love and acceptance, it would be from her. If I'd had any respect for her or myself, I'd have recognized the unhealthy basis for our relationship. She, too, would have recognized the unhealthiness of the relationship if she had any respect for herself. Both of us had growing to do as individuals. I admit that I probably had more growing to do.

During our on periods, I was not happy either, though. My ego would inflate, and I'd think I could do better. I'd pick her apart as a person as to why she's not good enough for me. The depression remained, just with different fuel. Worse still, I remained incapable of being my true self. I lacked bravery, confidence, and the ability to face rejection. Even with Kayleigh, who would have loved me through anything, I could not show my truest self. She knew me better than anyone, yes, but not the true me. I still held back.

Why was I so unhappy? My life had turned into a treasure hunt, seeking out any false acceptance I could find. I'd run from one girl to the next. Wandering. When I got acceptance, it felt good - for a little while. Then it got stale, and I moved on. I gathered up enough courage to tell them of the diapers, but not nearly enough courage to show my true spirit to them. I'd fallen into the trap of over-identifying with diapers, believing acceptance of diapers is acceptance of me. Unaware, I wasn't after any real relationships. I was only after the acceptance, and even that was fake as I refused to show my true self. This is not a good life to live. I wouldn't recommend it to anyone. I was never truly happy, and I now know I never could have been. Not that way.

What was my type of woman? One that liked me. There were no traits that were deal breakers. I gravitated towards women who were as broken as I was. Any mentally healthy woman would see me for the cancer I was. This is not a self-depreciating statement. I was not a good boyfriend for anyone! I had no concern for their needs. I did not want to give. My only concern was to get my fix of illusory acceptance and belonging. I never, ever, asked a girl out. I was not worthy, nor prepared to face rejection. The only girls I ended up dating would hit on me. I never "made a move" on a girl. She would make the first move, or it wouldn't happen. Many relationships ended because I never made a move, and they were left to assume I was not attracted to them. I never, ever, broke up with a girl. I was not worthy. Relationships only ended when *she* decided it was over. If I wanted out of the relationship, rather than break up with them, like a man, I would drop hints as to why it wasn't going to work out, or resort to flat out rudeness, practically daring them to break up with me. I never felt like I was good enough to date them, anyway.

*   *   *

Around my mid-twenties, I dated a nurse with a young child. I stayed at her place now and then. One morning, she woke me up in a panic. "I have to go to work *now!* It's an emergency! You have to take care of Ben."

I was scared. I still believed that my parents were right in branding me a child molester. I figured I didn't have much choice in the matter, and I'd do my best to maintain self-control. I didn't want to be a child molester, so I would simply choose not to. I agreed to watch him while she was gone.

He woke up. I changed his diaper, got him dressed, fed him breakfast, sat him down in front of some cartoons. All was well. The concern for his well-being was intense, while the intent to harm him or molest him was non-existent. It was that day I realized that I was not a child molester.

There was no sexual interest in children. The funny feelings I got when I saw kids in diapers were not of sexual attraction, but jealousy. Baby diapers are awesome, far better quality and much cuter than even the best adult diapers. Babies get to wear diapers everywhere, and are lovingly changed and cared for. I think that at the core of Adult Babies' drives is this desire to live as a child, to be diapered, unjudged, unconditionally loved and accepted, and cared for. My worry and guilt of thinking I may have been a molester (or would be some day) instantly transformed into anger towards my mother for putting the thought into my head. It still shocks me to consider the mental and emotional damage my parents instilled within me in the name of what's good for me.

*   *   *

As time progressed, I found more and more acceptance, if you can call it that, yet I became more and more unhappy. I was getting frustrated, which became a good thing, resulting in a realization that what I was doing wasn't working. A change was inspired. Tony Robbins accurately calls it the pain-threshold, when the pain or frustration gets so great that a change must occur. I hit the first pain-threshold at twenty-six and more were to come.

My answer was to settle down with Kayleigh. This was an improvement. The wandering was not productive. I learned to appreciate Kayleigh a bit more and our relationship became better. It went well for a few years. We even started counseling and began working on our individual selves during this time. The counselor we got was awful, though. Her answer was "You just have to love yourself and everything will be better." Wow, doc. Thank you so much for this wonderful insight. No further instruction or explanation is needed. I paid a hundred bucks a week to be instructed to love myself! It was frustrating because this was not my issue. I already knew that I needed to love myself. The problem was that I didn't know *how* to love myself. Kayleigh, too, had this problem. I was not too keen on working on it together. I never opened up to anyone like that, and I wasn't about to put myself in that vulnerable a position with anyone, even Kayleigh.

The counselor's instructions were daily affirmations. Look yourself in the eyes in the mirror and say to yourself "I love you, just the way you are." Over time, she said, you'll start to believe it. The mere thought of doing this, however, brought up a deep, dark rage reminiscent of my teen years. I hated myself. I didn't like being in the room with myself. Looking in the mirror just reminded me who I was, and I hated who I was! I mean, I really, truly, deeply, and angrily hated myself. Looking in the mirror was not an option. Telling the reflection he was loved was a lie on both ends of the mirror. The speaker was lying, and the listener was sure that he was not worthy of love.

The counselor did not work out. After a few years, the relationship between Kayleigh and me became troubled as our own personal issues caught up with us. There were two significant events that led up to the end of our relationship and the biggest period of growth I ever could have imagined.

First, I did something behind her back. As I said, I sought out acceptance, and from Kayleigh, it was guaranteed. This feeling was nice, but fleeting. I just wanted more. I think that what I really wanted was full acceptance from everybody, and my plan was to get it one person at a time. I'd been with Kayleigh steadily for a couple years, and I found myself wanting more attention. Kayleigh provided adequate attention and acceptance, but I wanted more, from more people. It was like a drug. Each time I got a hit of acceptance, I was relieved, but shortly thereafter, it would wear off, and I'd seek more. As my twenties progressed, the satisfaction I got from each person's so-called acceptance lessened, as did the time until I wanted more.

Besides, I thought, Kayleigh could never understand me because she was not into diapers like I was. It is a rare person that can relate to being five years old and hungrily scanning the Sunday newspaper ads for diaper pictures, coupons, and sales.

Kayleigh and I had been doing well. Life was good. Inside, though, I was not happy. Kayleigh's affection was great, but I needed more! So I looked for more by way of Craigslist. I posted an ad asking for some diaper attention. Maybe someone could change me? Maybe some fondling could take place? I didn't really want the sexual aspects. I felt like it would sweeten the deal. I needed attention in diapers to give me the illusion of acceptance, but what was I offering in return? I offered that level of sexuality to entice potential applicants into changing me.

Man, woman, I didn't care. I liked women, but I was with Kayleigh, and I wouldn't cheat on her. I felt that since I was not attracted to men, attention from men was safer. It's not cheating if it's with a man, as I am not homosexual, or so went my logic. I needed attention in diapers. From whom was not important.

Long story short, one guy was into ABs, or was curious about a guy in diapers, and expressed interest in changing me. Kayleigh was sick that night. I told her I was running to the store, and she specifically asked why I was taking along with me so many adult diapers. I insisted I was just refreshing my stash in the car. (You never know when you need a change whilst out on the town.) I felt like I wasn't lying because I was, in fact, going to the store. It was a lie of omission. I went to the guy's apartment. He invited me in, and I sat on his couch. We chatted for a minute. Eventually we broke through the awkwardness and he asked if I needed a change. He laid a towel on the couch under me, and I removed my shorts, sitting in only a diaper and a t-shirt. I'll spare the intimate details, but my diaper was changed, there was indeed fondling, and it resulted in orgasm.

I left in a comfy fresh diaper, but ashamed and unsatisfied. What's worse, I couldn't figure out why. I did this behind Kayleigh's back, and I didn't even enjoy it! What was my problem?! The self-hatred and anger boiled.

Only days later, she confronted me about it. I seem to remember her searching my email or something to that nature, and I confessed. If she directly asked, I had to answer. I prided myself for not being a liar. Ironic, I know, that I was far from honest. I conned myself into believing that as long as I didn't directly say a falsehood, I was an honest person. She did ask, and I did honestly answer. She did not take it well. Surprised? Suddenly, it *did* feel like cheating, and I felt ridiculous that I convinced myself otherwise beforehand.

Her trust in me was broken. Things were rough in the relationship for months, but they settled after a time. Her trust never did restore, though. On one hand, I feel awful for putting her through that. On the other, though, I can see now the unhealthy lifestyle I was trapped in to which I was utterly oblivious at the time. I was just trying my best to live, but lacked the solid foundation necessary to make the proper decisions. By now, I have no guilt. I have come to terms with my poor decision making skills in my past. I don't regret it, necessarily. Rather, I accept it as natural actions from the confused state I was in. Mistakes, poor choices, and failures are only negative if we don't learn from them. I want to tell my story, as difficult as it is at times, so that others can learn from my failures and enjoy richer lives.

Despite this event, and her lost faith in me notwithstanding, we stayed together dating. Over a year had passed, and the second significant event transpired.

I was on vacation. Kayleigh had to work and was unable to join me, so I was on a solo road trip to visit a friend. On the third night, Kayleigh called, having searched my email again. This time, it was not about me seeking out other attention on Craigslist. Rather, I was in email communication with another woman.

This girl and I had become email pen pals long, long before. I was sixteen when I first met her online, and we got along really well. I ended up visiting her a couple times when I was eighteen for a go at a romantic relationship, but it fizzled somewhat quickly due to the long distance in between. Still, we remained email friends for years to come. It was a nice friendship to have. I could really pour my soul out to her and not worry about judgment. I was a similar outlet for her. I was able to be myself in those emails. My goofy, emotional, flirtatious self.

It's that flirtatious part that was the problem. Kayleigh checked my email. She already had reason not to trust me. She read an email with my email pen pal, sensed a flirtatious vibe, and confronted me about it. I was in a different city, and it didn't seem like the type of thing we could hash out over the phone, but I was able to talk with the friend I was visiting about my issues. It got deep. I really confronted some demons that night. The most memorable moment was when he asked me if I loved anyone at all. I thought about it, and said "no." He responded, "of course not! How could you love anyone if you don't love yourself? I can't imagine what that feels like."

I honestly was not into my pen pal. I was content with Kayleigh. I also don't find anything inherently wrong with some flirtation outside of a relationship. This is a common difference between men and women. If I'm being completely honest, though, I would have to admit that on some level, I was keeping that option open in the future. Understandably! If things were to not work out with Kayleigh, where would I get my acceptance fix? Keeping options open, I think, is the true purpose for this external flirtation in men, although they are mostly not aware of it.

It was that night with my best friend that I decided I was going to do something about it. I have lived my entire life, as long as I can remember, feeling like a loser, inferior, unworthy, angry, resentful, and flat out hating myself to pieces. I always knew this wasn't healthy or normal, but I never knew what to do about it. I never knew what was wrong with me. It was that night that I decided that I would fix this problem. Or, at least I would start thinking about planning to study my options to attempt to consider the possibility of changing. I was absolutely convinced that things would get a whole lot worse before they got any better, and I was not certain of a positive outcome. This scared me, and prevented me from committing 100% right away. This can still be considered a pain-threshold, but it didn't inspire active change. The thought process the event inspired, though, was certainly a push down the proper path.

Kayleigh and I went back to that bad counselor. I didn't know how little help she was providing as I hadn't yet experienced a good counselor. It was the same old stuff. "Just love yourself." Deciding to change, though, was changing my life for the positive, however slight. To be fair, the counselor did give me one piece of helpful advice. She told me that if I can't love myself, love my inner child. Now this I could relate to!

I imagined a clone of me that was nine years old. He was exactly like me. He struggled socially the way I did, he thought the same things I did, treated people the same way I did, made the same decisions I did, enjoyed the same things - like diapers - that I did, and believed the same things I did. I felt nothing but love and compassion for this imaginary child. Why, then, was I so hateful towards myself? Why the double standard? Why couldn't I look at myself the same way I looked at others? Even after these realizations, I found myself loving the imaginary kid, and simultaneously hating myself, fully aware of the contradiction! I kept reminding myself that that kid was me! It helped - a little.

Kayleigh and I never recovered. At the time, I blamed the two incidents; the cheating incident and the email. Really, there was only one thing to blame, and that was that we both were not healthy individuals. We reached a level of maturity at which we can no longer get our gratification from external sources. I make it sound so mature and civil. In real life, there was a lot of shouting and yelling and judgment.

I wanted to break up with her for months, but I couldn't. I did not feel worthy to end a relationship. I knew how depressed I became when I was single. If I broke up with her, then I was to blame. No, I was much too proud for that. If I could get her to break up with me, though, then I would still be depressed and single, but not by choice. (I know it is irrational.) Therefore, I simply explained to her why this relationship should not continue, and hoped that she would break up with me. Then I could play the victim. She never did, though. She needed me as much as I needed her. Of course, what we *really* needed was to be on our own journeys of self-discovery, but this was beyond us. The fighting continued until finally, one night, she yelled at me for hours over something entirely inconsequential. A female coworker had brought me dinner to work for my birthday. Innocent enough, but you can't blame Kayleigh. The events of our past, and our inner demons, provided the foundation for insecurity.

I couldn't break up with her because, as bad as things were now, things would be much worse alone, with nobody to provide that acceptance I needed so badly. But the fighting and yelling continued for hours, and we weren't getting anywhere. I realized, then, that the fighting was not about an issue, but about the very core of our relationship. I'd grown so tired and miserable in the relationship that I no longer feared the potential pain of being single. At that time, days after my thirtieth birthday, for the first time in my life, I broke up with my girlfriend. She fell silent and left the room. I didn't look at it as a good thing or a bad thing. I was relieved it was over, but fearful of the future of single life. I fell right asleep pretty quickly that night.

The next day, she apologized. She admitted that she was out of line yelling at me, and maybe we can give it another go. But I saw something that she didn't, that our relationship, as desperate as we needed it, was hurting us more than helping us. I had become so miserable in the relationship that I still did not want to go back to it. I would rather face the abyss of being single. Already my mind had moved on to forming a plan to get another girlfriend to fill the void. How could I trick someone into loving me for a little bit? I'd have to present myself in such a manner that they're tricked into accepting the diaper side of me. So, so stupid.

*   *   *

The relationship was over, and I was alone. I sank into a deep, dark depression. Those thoughts that it would get worse before it got better stuck with me, though. The easy way out - that is, getting back together with Kayleigh - was no longer an option. I was ready for a better life in which I respected myself. So I endured the depression. It was early 2011, and I made a decision. I was sick and tired of feeling this depressed. I've carried this depression with me my entire life. Sure, it was worse now because of the breakup and my decision to beat it, but it'd always been with me. I didn't always admit it, or acknowledge it, but it was always there. I'm not carrying it with me anymore. I swore that 2011 was the year I would beat my depression. If I couldn't do it on my own by midyear, I would get professional help. If I couldn't do it with help by the end of the year, I would get on anti-depressants, which I'd always avoided.

With this goal in mind, I went forth into 2011. I didn't know what to do exactly, but I tried each day to be happy. My imaginary nine year old clone was with me often. He helped, but I did not make any real progress.

In March, I broke down and found me a girlfriend online. The depression was too hard. We dated for a month or so, got along well enough. One day, she started acting weird. That happened to me often in past relationships. I'd become a nervous wreck. "What did I do wrong?" "Was it something I said?" *I'm such a loser!*

A couple days later, we had a talk. She asked me why I liked her. My first instinct, "Well, because you like me!" I didn't say it out loud, though. I never said the first thing that came to mind. It went through a "what will make her like me" filter. That filter held back the real me.

I said "You're nice, you're sweet" along with a whole other load of crap. The characteristics were all true – she was a total sweetheart - but they were not the reasons I liked her. My type was whoever liked me at the time.

"Huh," she said, then paused. "Are you sure it's not because I like you?"

She called me out! Still, I denied profusely. "That's ridiculous! That would not be a good reason to like anyone," I said. I was trying to convince myself more than her. I was in denial. I was not ready to face that fact. Not yet. She knew though. She knew damn well that I was with her for the wrong reasons.

The next day she broke up with me. It was the right decision for her. I'm impressed she could see through my façade. I guess healthy people have a way of sensing a person's false portrayal of self. Still, I needed some type of reassurance. I remember during the discussion in which she broke up with me, I said "You probably think I'm some sort of jerk." She assured me she did not, but the question really shows how emotionally needy I was.

*   *   *

So I was back to square one. Still trotting my way through 2011, depressed, but ready to fight. I knew that the depression was not caused by lack of girlfriend, but something much deeper. I knew I was not ready for a relationship, and that seeking one out was my weakness getting the better of me. I recommitted.

Still, happiness didn't come. I remained deep in depression. I told myself to be happy, but my depression was stubborn. Kayleigh and I talked now and then when some sort of business needed to be handled. Much of our finances were intermingled, so we couldn't very well pretend we didn't exist. During one of these conversations, I was telling her how depressed I was, and she reminded me that it was about time to get that professional help, as I was clearly not making any progress on my own. It was true.

It was a month earlier than planned, but I started asking around for a *good* psychologist. I was willing to pay for help as long as it helped. The best recommendation came from my mother, whose psychologist friend insisted this guy was the best.

Knowing full well it would get much worse before it got better, I began seeing this guy weekly. Sitting in the waiting room before my first appointment, I skimmed through a Psychology Today article that mentioned coming out in the work place. It stressed the idea that self-worth must come from within. The timing was great, because I didn't know what I was going to tell this guy, and the magazine put it so well.

Dr. Rush called me in, and first thing, he asked what I expected to get out therapy. I'd carried the magazine into the room with me, and read the line verbatim. Summed up, I want this so-called self-worth.

And so it began. I talked, and he stopped me when I was saying something defeating, like "this is who I am." You hear it, and maybe you say it, all the time. I never knew the damage it causes.

I'm not saying that it helped me immediately. On the contrary, I was flat out pissed at this guy after the first session. What an ass! He doesn't know me, and he doesn't know anything! Or so was my attitude after the first visit. The anger was intense, but it faded. During the week, no change.

Still, I returned. After the second visit, I was crying. I was so frustrated. I didn't understand anything he was saying. I felt beyond help, far too broken for his assistance.

It wasn't until the fourth visit, four weeks in, that he finally broke through to me. He said I was denying my feelings, and what I should do is accept and feel my feelings as they carry messages important to me. Negative feelings tell me I'm doing something wrong or I'm thinking something wrong. This fourth visit was not the first time he said this, mind you. This time, though, I got frustrated. I didn't understand it! What was he trying to tell me! I shouted at him, "Well, what the hell is being depressed all the time trying to *tell* me?! What's the message there?!"

Instantly, he responded, "The message is that your thinking sucks!"

Oh. Suddenly it made sense. Why it sunk in this time and not the first three times, I do not know. I notice the pattern often, though. I liked that he spoke my language. It was direct. He said it with a chuckle, like it was so blatantly obvious, and it was, to him. The tone was necessary to break through my stubbornness. Fact is, I was clinging to my depression as part of "who I was." This was the first breakthrough to true recovery. Heck! Forget recovery. I was on the road to true happiness.

It did get worse before it got better, but it was not what I expected. It got only slightly worse for only a very short period, then became better than I could have imagined. Not overnight, of course. After that fourth visit, I started having more good days, and each week, I had more good days and less bad days. I was gaining confidence daily and learning to respect myself.

One night at work, I was chatting with a few customers and entertaining them, making jokes and laughing. They were having a great time, and so was I. All was well, and I was feeling swell. Then it was break time. As I walked away, I caught a glimpse of my reflection in the window. I felt so charming and charismatic a few seconds ago with those people, but that was not the person I was looking at in the mirror. That guy was a goofy looking, nerdy, goobery loser. I hate that guy. And instantly, my mood changed. I was down the rest of the night. I remained down the rest of the week, but that I was feeling good at all early on was a sign of improvement, and it would be a matter of days until I could address this incident in therapy.

"It's your ego," he explained. "Your ego compares and judges. We all have an ego, just accept it for what it is. It holds no truth." Basically, I had to stop giving so much credit to my thoughts, as they were just thoughts, not facts.

We talked a lot about who I was. The statement "this is who I am" was off limits. He insisted that was *not* who I was. "Well, who am I, then?"

This is the ultimate question. Who am I? This is the key to happiness.

*   *   *

I had been visiting my psychologist for a couple months and was feeling good. Really good, in fact. I was experiencing life in an entirely new way. The first time I noticed it was with my best friend at a restaurant. He asked the waitress what she would recommend, and I made a joke about how he didn't want to do that because you couldn't possibly trust a waitress. Nathan gave me a weird look, and I thought, "Oh crap! That could have been really offensive to her!" Then, "Here comes the depression." Normally when I did something stupid, it was followed by a wave of self-hatred and depression that would last for weeks. But the depression didn't come. I was ready for it, poised for it, but there was nothing. Instead, I thought to myself "Well, I'll have to be more careful about what I say in the future." Then, the most amazing thing happened. I continued my day in a good mood, maintaining the inner peace I had before. This may seem like a mundane story, but it was one of the most significant experiences in my life. This had never, ever happened to me. It felt so foreign and unnatural, but so very welcome. The excitement! Was this how the rest of my life was going to be? Is this what life is like with a little bit of self-love?

That wasn't all. Experience after experience, I was amazed at how confident I was and how capable I was of flourishing in social situations! The entire world was new, like I was experiencing it for the first time. I felt like I was exploring a brand new planet. Words cannot compare the before and after. It was, without a doubt, the most exciting time of my life.

I started dating Kayleigh again. It wasn't like before. I wasn't after some cheap acceptance fix. We started talking one day in the midst of my self-improvement, and I realized that Kayleigh was an amazing person, the kind of woman that I'd been searching for, and I never got to appreciate her in this way. After a decade of dating, it wasn't until now that we really got to know each other. It wasn't until this point that we could truly show ourselves to each other. During this time seeing each other, I had never been happier with her in the past. However, even in the healthiest state we'd ever dated in, I could still see that she was not for me. It was an amazing experience. I'd never gotten to know anyone like that before. We learned more about each other in those six weeks of dating than in the past ten years. It was also gratifying to know that ultimately we did not end up together not because of our immaturity, poor timing, or internal issues, but because we just were not that compatible. Six weeks in, she started seeing someone else and it was over. Amazingly, life went on.

Her new boyfriend became a great ally. She talked to him about my issues, and he could relate well. His thing was not diapers, but cross dressing, but went through the same self-loathing issues that I went through and, by way of Kayleigh as an intermediary, gave me some valuable coaching that I truly appreciate. He recommended two books: <u>Awaken the Giant Within</u>, by Tony Robbins; and <u>The Power of Now</u>, by Eckhart Tolle.

While it took four weeks to make my first significant breakthrough with my psychologist, things accelerated beyond that. It was only ten weeks in that I felt ready to drop down to one visit every other week. After just a few of those, I dropped it down to monthly. I was doing well, loving life, and experiencing the world anew. I met a girl I liked. She seemed like she had some issues, and it worried me that I might be falling into my old habits of finding girls as broken as I was, but she was a fascinating person nonetheless. She was intelligent, passionate, and interesting. I gathered up the courage to tell her that I was interested in her, foreign territory for me, mind you. I told her about the diapers, but not for the acceptance this time. I told her so she could make an informed decision whether to have a relationship with me. Or, so I thought. She rejected me, citing that my diaper fetish was a sign of deeper, more troubling issues, which she was not prepared to handle. "Here comes the depression." I thought. Only this time, it did come. It hit me like a tidal wave.

This depression lasted a long time. I thought I was doing well, but there I was, right back to where I was a year ago. I supposed that the progression I'd made in the past few months was illusory. I must have just lied to myself that I was doing well and that I was happy, because this one thing happened and I'm right back in the depth of depression.

"No," my psychiatrist explained when I finally saw him again. "The sooner you realize that you will slip up, the easier your life will be. Face it. You're going to make mistakes. You're human. It's inevitable. If you think you're not, you're just lying to yourself. You are going to slip up, so be prepared to catch yourself. Awareness is key. As soon as you feel yourself slipping, catch yourself and correct your course." Just like that, I felt better. I thought I learned everything I needed from therapy, but this proved to be one of the most necessary sessions of all. Had I not learned this, I very well could have been back where I started. I am forever grateful.

*   *   *

The end of the year was nigh. I had accomplished what I set out to do. Anti-depressant drugs would not be necessary. I was growing beyond the need for therapy. I was finishing up <u>Awaken the Giant Within</u>, which helped me gain control over my life. I started dating someone new. For the first time of my life, age thirty, I made the first move. I avoided rejection my entire life, and in doing so avoided anything great. Now, rejection wouldn't ruin me. Rejection wouldn't send me into depression. My self-worth came from within, and no rejection could bring me down. But rejection didn't come. It was the first girlfriend I *chose* to be with. I'd never dated someone whilst maintaining the power to leave at any moment and knowing I'll still be fine. I didn't stay with her because I needed her. For the first time of my life, I dated her because I *wanted* her. What a novel idea.

Something was bothering me, though. I was feeling good. Happy. Joyful. I would go so far as to say I had inner peace. I knew it wasn't immovable, though. I learned that a few months prior with my depression relapse. So, what was the difference? What made me happy and content now that I lacked before when I was sad and lonely? What was it? The only answer I could come up with was a hundred-or-so-part-answer consisting of all the little quips that my psychologist had mentioned through my months of therapy. Each one was valuable and life changing, and combined, they made up that body of knowledge that transformed me from the old, depressed Brian to the new and improved, happy

Brian. What, though, was the underlying theme? What did they all have in common?

The problem was that if I were to "slip up" in the future, as he assured me I would, I couldn't very well remember each of the hundred-or-so memes he recited in therapy, could I? What I wanted was one underlying theme to remember that embodied all of those truths. Unfortunately, this is life. Life is not black and white. Things aren't always wrapped up in a nice little package. No. I'd have to come to terms that there was no underlying theme, and I'd just do my best to remember whatever gems I needed in whatever unpleasant situation I might find myself in the future. Such is the complexity of life.

The Power of Now cleared things up for me. It, too, was a collection of numerous quips entirely useful, but had a much more precise underlying them. The theme was: Who am I?

Who am I? This is the ultimate question. This is your key to inner peace. It's the most difficult question to answer, and holds a greater reward than any other piece of knowledge.

Every visit to my psychologist, he'd say "that's not who you are." I'd say I like scrabble. "That's not who you are." I wear diapers. "That's not who you are." I am a really nice person. "That's not who you are." I am six feet of ruggedly handsome, yet boyish good looks. "That's not who you are."

"Then who the hell am I?" I finally shouted.

"I can't answer that for you." Yeah. A lot of help you were, Doctor.

Only now that I know who I am do I understand. My psychologist was right. You can't be told who you are. You can be told who you're not, and you can be told how to find out who you are. Only you can find your true self. The reason for this is that your true self is deep, deep within you. Beyond your body, beyond even your mind. Who you are is not your thoughts, and your thoughts are not who you are. This idea sounded crazy to me. I have to be my thoughts, I thought. But then I thought... look who's telling me that. This is a silly way of explaining something so profoundly true. These thoughts to which I'm referring are from the ego, and our ego clings to judgments, belongings, and false identities in order to separate ourselves from everyone else. Our true selves come from what we share with everyone.

I could talk forever about the importance of finding your true self. I could write an entire book about finding your true self, but Eckhart Tolle already has one. This book is about Adult Babies, and I've mentioned diapers seldom in the past few pages. The point is, I found myself, and things became clear.

THE NEW BRIAN

I don't care so much about what people think of me. Good or bad, it does not matter. Someone likes Old Brian, he's happy. Someone dislikes Old Brian, he's depressed. What people think doesn't matter to New Brian. It does not say anything about me. Rather, it says something about their biases. To have biases is human, not God.

Old Brian would try to impress, and even still, some people wouldn't like me. The people that did like me, in reality, liked this character that I created in attempt to impress! So, why not be my true self, and achieve the same results in which some people will like me and some will not? Same results, except that the people that like me truly like the real me!

So, this begs the question, why not come out as an Adult Baby? Why don't I just walk around every day to the park and the grocery store and karaoke night in my shortalls and diapers?

Look, I'm human, I am far from perfect. I don't have all the answers. I still struggle with things. I am sorry if you expected a guidebook to life with all the answers, because I do not have them. I am still learning life. If I don't fear what others think, then why not just walk around in baby clothes all day? Well, a part of me fears that I would offend people. But that's not really a good reason, is it? Even when I was the people pleaser, still sometimes people would be offended. I could say something entirely positive and it's possible someone would get offended.

Being offended happens within one's own mind. What happens in our minds exists nowhere else. It's literally made up. If I do something, and someone is offended, that happens in their minds. I don't have control over that, they do! If they voice their opinion, and I feel bad, *that* is what happens in my mind, and I do have control over feeling bad.

If no matter what I do I run the risk of being offensive, then the only clear answer is to be my true self.

I am certain that at least one person out there is going to be offended by this book. That person is only offended by my true self. This book is my direct, pure expression of the truest me. That they might be offended will not change me as a person. I am who I am for a purpose. The proof is in my existence. To pretend to be someone I'm not is like telling God (or nature, or the universe, or whatever gives you life—let's not get hung up on semantics) that He got it wrong. That's absurd! You are an expression of nature. You are an expression of God! You are exactly who you are meant to be! That some other mere human being doesn't *like* who you are does not invalidate your being one little bit. Therefore, to be your true self is far more important than living a non-offensive life.

Fact is, I do occasionally go out in my baby clothes. I am surprised by the reactions, or lack thereof. People stare, but look away if I glance their direction. People that talk to me are overly professional as not to offend. We're so politically correct these days that to address a difference is considered hating a difference. Nobody has ever asked me about what I'm wearing. Ever. One time, a car full of teenagers pointed and laughed. I felt better about that interaction than any other because at least they acknowledged that something was different! It's not that I need the acknowledgement. What bothers me is knowing how uncomfortable everyone else is with themselves. They are too afraid to offend me that they can't ask about the get up, and you know they want to. Curiosity and interest in others is completely natural. It's not every day you see a grown man in baby diapers sucking on a pacifier. If one were offended, so be it.

My entire life, I sought out acceptance from others. I needed that validation, because I felt worthless on the inside. I kept searching, often in desperate and entirely unhealthy situations, like among strangers from the internet, and it never was satisfying. Veritably, the only acceptance that matters, the only love that matters, the only worthiness that matters, comes from you to you. If you don't love yourself, no amount of love from anyone else will ever truly fulfill you, and you'll live a life of perpetual chasing as I did.

As I became, or rather, as I am becoming more comfortable with myself, my life gets better and better. I experience true happiness all the time. I may have sadness some days, but I maintain inner peace on deeper levels. Before I'd have happy days, but I was still depressed on the inside. Some relationships I have lost, which turned out to be a good thing. They were friends with the fake me I'd been acting like. Losing those pseudo-friends was a minor hiccup compared to the rich friendships that have developed since then. I hold nothing back. I say what's on my mind, I'm more creative, and I feel more powerful and in control that ever before.

*   *   *

My relationship with my mom has gotten better. In my late twenties I told her that I was trying to be more open about diapers, and she told me that it would be best if I kept it hidden to respect that others might not be so comfortable about it. That was before my Big Change, what I call my transformation at age thirty from depressed and lost to confident and enlightened, or at least on my way to enlightenment. Recently, though, I told her that I was going to be more open, and explained that I cannot help who I am and I refuse to hide it any longer, and she accepted. I believe that the second time it was coming from a better, truer place, leaving no room for argument.

In a recent conversation with her, I mentioned my guilt for being such a bad child and giving my parents such a bad time. She looked at me, shocked, and asked me if I really thought that I was a bad kid, to which I replied "of course." She then took on a pained expression and insisted that I was a great kid and not at all bad.

I had never really considered it before, but I was not bad. As a child, I wanted nothing more than to be good, follow the rules, and be loved by my parents. All I remember, though, was being yelled at daily, feeling guilty for doing things behind their backs and breaking the rules, and life under perpetual grounding. It's no wonder I recalled being a bad kid because I was persistently treated like a bad kid. Upon this realization that I was not a bad kid, the most heart wrenching epiphany of my adult life, I mourned my childhood, forever lost. A more experienced writer might be better able to communicate the deep sadness and melancholy this experience conjured within me.

What about my relationship with my dad? I was not comfortable spending time with him because I felt like we were both pretending that our past didn't happen. We grew apart. He would only call on my birthdays, and maybe we'd meet up for lunch or dinner the following week. Time passed, and I eventually stopped answering those calls. Then he stopped calling even on my birthday. I didn't care for a relationship with him because he didn't accept me. It seemed that he was indifferent about having a relationship with me. So why put myself through the stress for some "obligation" that fathers and sons should have relationships?

New Brian looked at it a different way, though. I realized that I was deciding for him that he didn't accept me, that he was pretending the past didn't happen, and that he didn't care if he had a relationship with me. A couple years passed with "call dad" on my "to do" list. Finally, he called for my thirty-third birthday, and I agreed to meet him. I addressed these issues, and what he said surprised me. He told me that what I should really be mad at him about is that he did not provide unconditional love to me growing up. I couldn't disagree. He does not like that I wore diapers and did his best as a parent at the time. That he hadn't yet learned to love himself, I can completely understand, made it difficult to provide a healthy environment for his children.

But the biggest shock was that he explained that he did not look at me as some freak that wore diapers. To me, diapers became a huge thing in my life, and essentially controlled my teenage years. It was a stressful enough time in my life that it became the way I looked at my dad, as an asshole. He told me that to him, his relationship with me was so much more than that. He was there when I was born. He rocked me to sleep as a baby. He rushed me to the hospital when I almost died when a button I'd attempted to eat off the carpet became lodged in my trachea. He taught me how to ride a bike. Essentially, he was there through my whole life, and the diaper portion was a small part of that. He looked at me as a whole person with whom he had a lifelong relationship. I looked at him as a controlling, abusive ass that refused to understand and accept me. This father-son relationship is still under construction.

I considered waiting until I was fully out, completely understood the social dynamics of coming out, repaired my relationship with my dad, and had my entire life pitch perfect before writing this book. Then I thought, *When will I ever achieve perfection?* The book would never be written. We are all works in progress, yet we all have wisdom to share. Share what you know, and learn from others, and we're all better off for it. Why doesn't it work like this all the time? Because people are stubborn, and refuse to be wrong, and refuse to allow others to be wrong. They're attached to their ideas, and refuse to change. Anyone that disagrees is "ignorant." Don't shut yourself down to the vast world of ideas and knowledge out there! You don't know everything! I guarantee that you are wrong about *some* things. It seems contradictory to be open to new ideas while being sure of who you are, until we remember that our ideas are not who we are! I am 100% sure that some of the things I'm 100% sure of are 100% wrong.

*   *   *

My dad was right. I AM so much more than diapers. Why is this such a significant part of my life? It is just one of a million traits I have, so why does it feel so much bigger than the others? I wrote this entire autobiography, and did I mention I play the guitar? Or that I write my music? What about my interest in film production? Did I mention the screenplay I wrote with a friend? Why not? Why am I not writing a book about these traits? It is true that my perception of my babyhood *is* inflated beyond its real significance! Let's explore why, shall we?

I am a firm believer that my affection for diapers is one of many different traits that make up the total of me, thus, it is of no greater or lesser significance than any other trait. Does being a scrabble geek keep me up at night, worrying about who might judge me for it? Of course not, so why does being an Adult Baby? The reasons are many.

First, it's not "normal", or as I like to put it, it's not common. The rarer traits tend to be more shocking to people. People tend to like what is familiar to them. In terms of evolution, we can see how this trait became a matter of survival. You are alive, so you can survive anything you've encountered before. Hence, familiarity equals survival. Anything new can be feared and attacked, because it may cause the death of you. A guy at the mall in baby clothes is hardly threatening, but our minds make connections that don't always make sense. (Like, for instance, my connection to diapers.) What is unfamiliar, our minds insist, is life threatening.

We tend to search for validation of ourselves externally. I can look around and with ease find others interested in a game of Scrabble. Finding others into diapers is not so easy. I must find a specialty group online for that. The rareness of this trait makes it more difficult for individuals to handle.

Being rejected for a common trait, like blonde hair, or enjoying Scrabble, seems shallow, while being rejected for a rare trait, like wearing diapers, seems perfectly reasonable and socially acceptable. In fact, to accept someone for such a rare trait is often what is socially rejected. Judging a diapered adult is no less outlandish than judging one for keeping the company of a diapered adult.

Second, this trait has been the cause of much turmoil in my past, while Scrabble has not. This has led me to equating diapers as a very big deal, and Scrabble as insignificant. That my own parents rejected me for wearing diapers, I imagine, contributes greatly to its bloated significance.

Third, my diaper related desires have been repressed for my entire life. I think that if Scrabble were taboo and wearing diapers was perfectly acceptable, the roles would be switched. I would think nothing of wearing diapers, but feel the need to hide my love of Scrabble, covering word games with a blanket of shame. In that parallel universe, I'm writing this book for others that also love to play Scrabble, and I would be comparing it to something normal, like our common love for diapers.

Put another way, we all, as humans, have drives. The drives in which we indulge reasonably become a natural part of our being, while the drives we deny do not go away, but fight back. There are parts of our being that must be expressed! Repression leads to obsession. Our minds are powerful. If we obsess over something, it becomes a significant part of our lives, good or bad.

Altogether, these conditions artificially expand one trait, giving us the illusion that it is far more significant than other traits. This illusion is based only on what people think, which is the very definition of "imaginary," and not based in real life. Deep down, every trait is an equal part of our being. This artificial inflation of a trait's significance is based upon things that don't even matter: others' opinions. The question becomes, is reality based on the collective minds of people, or does reality transcend our perception?

I believe it is the latter. Reality is made up of trillions of stars and galaxies, while humans make up a miniscule portion. That we put such great value on one little person's opinion is laughable in this sense. If humans disappeared, reality will persist. Reality is not based on human perception. That our judged traits become inflated is mere illusion.

*   *   *

As for my relationship with my dad, I think back to my relationship with him through my entire life. I have a hard time remembering anything aside from the torture I got for wearing diapers. At our recent lunch meeting, he revealed an entire relationship, of which diapers was a small part. I have difficulty seeing it that way. I think of the influence he had on me. I remember him helping me with my homework one night and telling me to make my nines differently. I took it as harsh, not constructive, criticism, but I make my nines his way to this day. We installed new struts on a Toyota Camry once. That gave me confidence to maintain my own car as an adult. I struggle to think of much else aside from getting yelled at for sneaking diapers into his house.

He requests that I think about how rich our relationship was compared to how insignificant the whole diaper thing was as a teenager, and in that way begin repairing our relationship. I told him that he should not get his hopes up in that matter. His best bet is to begin anew and perhaps have a positive influence on me from this point forward. I do not cling to the past, nor resent it, nor dwell on it, but to change our past relationship from a negative influence to a positive seems unfeasible.

My father is missing a key point expressing the insignificance of diapers. It may be true that our relationship from the day I was born was far richer than what I remember it as. Yet, true acceptance of a child can only come in one form, and that form is universally. If a father rejects a small part of his son, a father rejects fully his son. If a father accepts 99% of his son, it is not true acceptance. What I recall from my pre-adult relationship with my father is one in which I was without the freedom to be myself. He is wrong. We may very well have had a richer relationship beyond diapers, but that became meaningless as he rejected this however small part of my being, and in doing so rejecting me fully.

*   *   *

I stopped seeing my Dr. Rush once I felt I could proceed on my own. We didn't talk about diapers directly that much. The conversations focused on self-worth, and diapers were a big part of the reason I had little, so in that sense, they were mentioned often. But his direct advice about diapers was to stop wearing them, for diapers are socially impractical and only causes problems. I agree it causes some issues, but I felt like he didn't quite understand the pull.

I did not choose to want to wear diapers. That desire within me is massive, and incredibly strong. I do choose to wear diapers. That much I have control over, although even that is somewhat arguable.

I ask myself often if I am addicted to diapers. My parents and the counselor I saw as a teenager insisted it was an addiction, and I ponder it often. It certainly acts like an addiction. Many times as a teen, I tried to stop wearing diapers, and every time I caved in. I felt guilty, anguish, remorse, shame, and regret, common emotions associated with relapse. With all the attempts to stop, I always came back.

What is an addiction? Webster's definition is "a strong and harmful need to regularly have something (such as a drug) or do something (such as gamble)". It's a peeve of mine to define a word in writing of it, but in this case it's entirely necessary. The key to an addiction is its harmful nature.

The only harm in wearing diapers is social harm. It is difficult to date and to be yourself without a strong likelihood of rejection. Yet, if we were to live our lives avoiding rejection, we set ourselves up for unfulfilling lives. I believe strongly that it is much more important to be true to yourself than to avoid social harm.

Painting is something an artist would be drawn to, no pun intended. If we were to take an artist's paint and canvas and denied him from creating, he would likely become depressed. He'd think about it all the time. He might sneak out at night to paint behind your back. Does that mean he's addicted to painting? Or, more likely, does it suggest painting is a part of his being?

Diapers do not cause harm unless we were to value shallow social harm. The artist's painting causes this type of harm if his parents want him to be a doctor and think art is a waste of time. Does that inherently make painting harmful? Hardly. This type of social harm should be disregarded.

It could be argued that wearing diapers is harmful in the form of rashes, financial harm (diapers are expensive!), or perhaps pollution levels. Even these can be compared to other habits that are commonly accepted, like eating meat, or cable TV. Even a day at the beech can cause skin damage worse than wearing a diaper.

As far as I can consider, I can think of no significant harm caused by wearing diapers that would categorize it as an addiction. I thank God that I was born with a drive that I can indulge in without causing harm to others! Could you imagine what it is like to live with a desire that did cause harm to others? I truly feel pity for cannibals, murderers, and even child-molesters. I have an intensely strong desire to wear diapers, and I can indulge without harm. The child-molester has an intensely strong desire to have sexual relations with minors, but to indulge is plain wrong. And this poor guy can't even get help without being branded a monster and locked up as a freak! This, however, is the subject of an entirely different book.

It's difficult to differentiate between the two, but I can say that from my perspective and deepest feelings, I consider the desire to wear diapers, and wearing diapers, as a part of my being rather than an addiction.

It's not all healthy, though. I am attached, and I believe all attachments are harmful to some extent, whether it is careers, appearances, relationships, habits, or items. Ultimately, none of these things define us. To become attached to any of them sets us up for an emotional whirlwind when we lose it. I say "when" rather than "if" because it is a fact that everything in our lives is temporary. Our truest selves will remain our truest selves without these things. I maneuver my way through this narrow realm by attempting to balance between indulging in diapers regularly (24/7, really), while maintaining my spiritual health as best I can to refrain from the attachment thereto. If some circumstances were to occur that resulted in no longer being able to wear diapers, as difficult as it may be, I will do my best to go on with strength and love and joy as before.

I now realize that this was what Dr. Rush was trying to tell me. He was not telling me to stop wearing diapers because it doesn't make sense. His message was much better, but at the time, I was not prepared to hear it. What he was telling me was to "make it a non-angst based choice. Don't wear them for some time, surrender to the discomfort, be without them in situations where you might be discontent with your internal state without diapers. Practice being without them, and let yourself feel what you feel." Through this process, the control that diapers have over me will be diminished. At that point, it's a non-angst based decision. Do I wear them or not? Either way, I am fine. Then the purpose of wearing diapers becomes clearer. It's functional or it's "taste", and not a matter of "ego" in some form or other. In other words, it becomes more of a conscious choice to wear diapers for pleasure, and not an unconscious attachment.

The fact remains that diapers do have control over me to some extent. This is what I find troublesome, and my long-term goals include taking back this control over my life. The process is intimidating, but necessary. Again, it would be nice if I had this all figured out before I decided to write a book. The book is published, but I am a work in progress.

EXAMINING MY PARENTS' ACTIONS THROUGH MY CHILDHOOD

I have learned much of myself and life in the past few years. One of the greatest realizations is that all hatred, anger, and non-acceptance is rooted in hatred, anger, and non-acceptance of oneself. I am confident that my parents gave me a hard time because they felt it reflected poorly on them. If their son turned out to be a diaper freak, the neighbors are going to think they're bad parents!

Did my parents love me? Well, as much as they were able to, I guess. They did not love themselves, and were therefore unable to love me.

When we're kids, we see the world split into two groups: adults and kids. The line is your 18th birthday, when you become an adult and, from then on, know everything. We are kids, we lack experience. They are adults, they know what they're doing. When I was young, I didn't decipher between a twenty year old and a fifty year old. They both were in the adult category.

As children, we have no choice but to rely upon the knowledge and wisdom of our parents. We look up to them, crave their acceptance and love, and live by their moral code. Once we cross that threshold into adulthood, we can see how far we still have to go. There is an entire world of growth in front of us. When I was twenty, I began seeing the difference in maturity, wisdom, and experience between twenty year olds and thirty year olds, but still saw little difference between thirty year olds and forty year olds. Now in my thirties, I see bigger difference between each of the age groups. I look at twenty year olds as more kids than adults, a thought that would have infuriated me when I was twenty.

My parents were in their twenties, though! They were just kids that I, as a young child, looked up to as adults who were supposed to have their shit together. Now that I know what it's like being an adult, I cut them some slack towards how they treated me. How they treated me was wrong, in my opinion, but I give them credit for doing their best and not knowing all the answers.

*   *   *

Fate is a funny thing. I am who I have become as a result of my life's experiences. Who we are is not what happens to us, but how we react. My life was difficult, and I was miserable for years, decades even. My childhood was tough, my teenage years were terrible, and in my twenties, I developed terribly unhealthy codependent habits. These became the basis for depression for my entire life, until at age thirty, I decided enough was enough. My life changed and improved, resulting in who I am today. Without the decades of pain, the hurtful experiences, the self-destructing habits, strenuous relationships, and my challenging quirk, I would not have journeyed into the self-defining territory to discover the strong, ambitious, confident, and boyishly handsome adult *and* Adult Baby I have become.

My story is rough. There have been difficult times. I'm well aware that others have had it far worse than I, which, in my twenties, contributed to more guilt for the depression I experienced.

I do not write for pity. I write for education.

I want struggling Adult Babies, and all people that are different, to know that there is a happy life for you out there. My goal is to empower these people. Learn from my mistakes, and borrow from my successes.

Second, Adult Babies are not bad people. Heck, I'm sure some are, but they are not inherently bad people. Do not judge me based on what you saw on Jerry Springer. Do not judge your Adult Baby friend based on my personal experience. We are all different. Each and every one of us is a unique, divine individual deserving of equal love and respect.

I want people in relationships with Adult Babies to learn who they are, and see that other people's differences do not reflect upon or affect who you are. Your actions can create new levels of love in your relationship, or cause tremendous harm in your and their lives. Please, learn from my parents' mistakes.

Lastly, to those that are neither Adult Babies nor close to one, there are lessons here for you, too. First, learn that we are all different. Your differences, whatever they may be, do not make you any worse, or any better, of a person. Learn to accept yourself, and you will be able to accept others. To judge for a quirk like wearing diapers is no more admirable than judging for the color of skin. Judgment is a universal wrong, like hatred. The direction of judgment does not validate the judgment.

*   *   *

I have concluded that I am not insane. It's hard to tell. Nobody that is insane knows that they are insane. However, I sympathize with others, have healthy relationships, and have healthy social interactions in my day to day life. Frankly, the most recognizable difference is my choice in underwear. Such an insignificant trait is not insanity.

I hope that my story can illustrate how an Adult Baby is not separate from you, but connected with you. I live life like anyone else. I struggle like everyone else. I have friends and dreams and problems like everyone else. That I grew up with an attraction to diapers makes me no less human than you.

It took a while, but I have come to terms with our differences.

Section 3:
How to live your life as an Adult Baby

Life is hard. Everyone in the world has different challenges to face on a daily basis. This becomes especially true to the misfits of the world. I use the word misfit literally, as someone that does not fit into the social expectations of the world. When a person, like myself, has drives to both wear diapers and have a healthy social life, he is faced with a choice to conform to society's expectations, or deny himself the pleasure of wearing diapers. Might there be a third option, in which he remains true to his own desires for his life *and* maintains a healthy social life? I have learned this to be entirely possible, and, in fact, much more satisfying on both fronts. The social interactions become more satisfying, as does life itself.

Let this section be your map, guiding you through the difficult territory that is life as an Adult Baby. Online, there is no shortage of photographs and drawings of men and women in diapers, nor is there a scarcity of discussions asking which adult diaper is the best and how to keep from getting "discovered". As an Adult Baby in my teens and twenties, I did not struggle with which diaper to wear, or where to hide them in my room.

I struggled with self-worth, depression, and social anxiety. Wearing a diaper, knowing that at some point I will have to tell the girl I'm dating, knowing that I am not like other people, and feeling different, strange, and insane were among my difficulties. Yet, there are no discussions on these subjects, and I am certain I am not alone in these difficulties.

There are occasionally some forum posts about wanting to tell one's parents or friends that they wear diapers, but the advice given leaves much to be desired. Mostly consisting of confused inquiries into why one would want to admit to something so disdainful, the replies are as unhelpful as they are discouraging of similar conversations in such forums.

This ends now. I am far from perfect, but I have faced the challenges others face, and I have emerged victorious on the other side. A guidebook through the difficulties of being an Adult Baby in a non-Adult Baby's world is necessary. I hope there is enough information within to point the way.

ARE YOU AN IMPOSTER?

Many of us are imposters. We walk around the world, living someone else's life. We go to work, make friends, date, and interact publicly not as ourselves, but as a character. We build this character based on what we think others want to see, what others will be attracted to, what bosses will hire, and what sexy people will love. We live our lives as imposters because we believe that if we were to live our lives as our true selves, we would not be attractive, admirable, hirable, loveable, or otherwise accepted.

There is a flaw in this thinking. Let's assume for a moment that the imposter is more likely to reap the benefits of social acceptance and examine the consequences. First, we doom ourselves to a lifetime of continuing the charade, lest we are exposed as the imposters we are. Second, any love, admiration, appreciation, or any other form of acceptance we receive is false. The joy in being loved is that *you* are being loved, not some character. We find that, living as an imposter, we glimpse this love and acceptance, but never experience it first hand in its richest, truest form. Lastly, and perhaps most significantly, we *still* face rejection! No human being is capable of creating a character that is so well liked that *everyone* likes them. Why do we insist on such a ridiculous practice with such poor results?

This book is not for happy people. While I'm sure there are plenty of happy people that may benefit from reading this book, the intended audience is an unhappy one, whom I intend to give instructions through the valleys of change and self-discovery, all the way to the peak of inner peace beyond.

Are you happy? Are you content? Do you feel that your being diapered is nobody else's business?   Do you not feel like an imposter? Then do not change.

We have emotions to guide us through our decisions. If we are happy and content, that is our bodies and/or souls communicating to us that we are doing something right. If we are miserable, depressed, and unsatisfied, that is our bodies and/or souls communicating to us that change must occur. For this reason, we must not deny or repress our feelings, but cherish them and welcome their guidance.

I write for the miserable people. I lay out my suggested changes that are likely to transform you into the self-loving, self-respecting, happy, peaceful, enlightened individual you have the potential to be. My authority on the subject is that I was once miserable and hated myself, and now I am happy and satisfied in life. More importantly, I have learned to love myself.

If you have no struggle with being an Adult Baby, then you truly have no reason to change.

Often in AB forums, one person will mention wanting to tell their friends, and inevitably, another will chime in with "Why the heck would you do that? It's none of their business." An argument often ensues. Why there is such a passionate difference in the way we want to live our lives, I do not know. To them, a guy like me who feels compelled to let the world know that I am an AB and proud of it is nothing short of insane and desperate. To me, guys like them who insist on keeping a portion of their life secret forever is akin to being an imposter, which is at best unfulfilling, and at worst, self-destructive.

Who am I to say that another's continued secrecy is unfulfilling? I am the first to admit that I do not hold that authority. It's obvious that we are all different people with different needs. I can't judge another for wanting to keep it secret any more than he can judge me for wanting it out in the open.

But it's not just disagreements in these forums. It can become downright hateful! Why is such aggression spewed my way at the mention of being my true AB self publicly? Fear. They believe that if I were to come out, it would bring attention to *their* abnormalities. I hold the belief that any lack of acceptance of another person stems from an internal lack of acceptance. Likewise, any outward hatred stems from internal hatred.

My values insist I live my life as myself. I can no longer be the imposter I impersonated for three decades. I've come to the belief that I am exactly who I am for a reason, and to be anything else is robbing myself of inner peace, and robbing the world of what only I uniquely have to offer. On a deeper level, I believe that I am as God made me, and to live as anyone else is equal to telling God that He got it wrong.

Many insist that as a sexual kink, wearing diapers should be held private. It's no more the public's business that he wears diapers than is his favorite sexual position. It is possible that this difference of opinion lies in how deeply ingrained diapers are into our being.

What of those that get no sexual gratification from wearing diapers, yet desire them still? Do they, then, have every right to come out? And what right does a homosexual have to come out, if that is a sexual attraction? For some, diapers are purely sexual, and for others, they satisfy so many other needs within us. I do not feel the need to tell my loved ones of the sexual endeavors I enjoy with my girlfriend, but diapers are far more than that to me.

Even if the only pleasure you got from a diaper *was* sexual, I would not label this as an invalid reason to be open about it. Modern culture shuns sexuality. We all have sexual desires, yet live our public lives pretending we have none. Regarding our choices, it would be irresponsible not to consider social consequences. Other people thinking negatively of you is meaningless.

Spending some time in jail is significant. A balance must be found. The ultimate question is: What is best for you?

The point is that you as the reader will have to make the decisions that guide your life on your own. You will make the decisions that you believe will be best for you. Most often, your internal compass points the way, but the courage to follow the direction is lacking. It is always easy for others to tell you how to live your life because they will not have to deal with the consequences. To decipher whether change is necessary, you need only basic self-examination. If you are happy and content, you needn't change a thing. If you are unhappy, discontent, or something feels "off" in your life, then something within you is telling you to change. Precisely what change is necessary, however, is more difficult to pin down.

In this section, I will explore many common social and internal difficulties associated with being an Adult Baby, and how I suggest they are handled based on my experience and results. Again, the decision is yours. My authority on the subject is that I am an Adult Baby that was miserable, made these changes, and am now happier than I ever thought I could be. I'm talking about a deep inner peace that is unshakable. We are all happy now and then, even the most miserable of us, but only you know if you are consistently truly happy on the inside, or if something is telling you to change.

WHY ARE WE LIKE THIS?

What made us so different? How can every one of our friends be perfectly content wearing their underwear and using the toilet? We all want so badly to be normal, so why aren't we? What has happened to us that makes us want to wear something intended for babies?

I spent much of my youth pondering this. I've searched for similarities among ABDLs. Do we all have younger siblings? Have we all had subpar childhoods? Late bloomers in potty training? Perhaps a result of some abuse? Is it a form of post-traumatic stress disorder, as has been suggested?

I never found the answer, but I did reach a conclusion by soul searching and self-examination.

The conclusion: It doesn't matter.

It doesn't matter why we are who we are. Wanting to know why is a trait of the ego, which constantly evaluates everything, desiring to understand the universe in as simple terms as possible. Life proves to be far more complex, and interesting, than we could realistically understand with our mortal human minds.

What is important, rather, is acceptance. You will probably never understand why you desire diapers, but what you're after in searching for causes and reasons is an illusory form of self-acceptance. By finding the causal root of our desires, we pass the blame of our abnormalities to nature. "Yeah, it's weird that I wear diapers, but it's not *my* fault. I didn't choose it. Something-or-other *happened* to me. It was beyond *my* control." Thus, the guilt of being different is relieved. It is convenient, I suppose, were it not entirely unnecessary, and gravely elusive.

Finding the sources of our behaviors has its place, but time spent on accepting the current situation will show greater payoffs.

"I THOUGHT I WAS THE ONLY ONE"

"I thought I was the only one." True and not true. You are not the only one that has the desire to wear diapers. We are many. But you are the only person that is you in the entire world. You are an individual, a direct expression of God, and you are you for a purpose. There is a reason for you being here that no other person on Earth can fulfil. In that way, you are indeed the only one.

THE BASICS

It's so easy to look at ourselves as different, as freaks. Different is a bland fact and has no "good" or "bad" associated with it inherently. The term "freak" is a word that can only make sense when compared to the term "normal", which itself is a concept society has made up to express what is common. Once we remove the biased opinions of fallible human beings, we can only conclude that our existence has purpose, and we are all equally valuable beings in the world, which brings me to the core value:

Learn to love yourself. This is a statement that is far easier said than done. First, you have to figure out who you truly are, and then you have to learn to love that person. This advice does not apply only to Adult Babies; in fact, the folks for whom Section 4 is intended must learn to love themselves as well. Likewise, any person in the world with an inner discontent must learn to love themselves.

Meeting your true self is no easy task. My self-discovering journey flourished with help from a psychologist, learning to meditate, and reading some thought inspiring books with incredible value, particularly The Power of Now, which I have since learned has inspired millions of others on their own journeys of self-discovery.

I do not want to go into too much detail on the hows of finding your true self, as there are already numerous books on the subject. Instead I want to make perfectly clear the intrinsic value of doing so. I strongly urge all seekers of truth to endure this difficult journey. Your spiritual wellbeing relies on it.

To embark, one option is to seek a good psychotherapist. The price can be a bit steep, but it was, hands down, the best money I have ever spent in my life.

Seek resources. There are numerous videos available online by Dr. Wayne Dyer, Kyle Cease, and more that can point you towards your true self. Eckhart Tolle's The Power of Now was especially helpful to me, as was Dr. Wayne Dyer's Change Your Thoughts, Change Your Life. I've heard numerous accounts of folks finding their true selves after reading Drama of a Gifted Child, by Alice Miller. There are hundreds of them. Find one that speaks to you.

Alternatively, try seeking within you. This is where the answers are, after all. All these books, videos, and therapists are only pointing the way. They give you a road map so that you can embark on the journey within. Is it possible to find yourself without the map?

Absolutely, it is. If weeks have passed and you make no progress, however, get yourself a map.

Yet, remember that the map, books, videos, and words are not the truth. It is like the old Zen Buddhist story in which a finger pointing to the moon represents the words, while the moon itself represents the truth. You don't see the truth looking at the hand, but beyond the hand to the moon. And the moon, or truth, was there all along.

*   *   *

I believe I would be doing my readers a disservice if I were to ignore the explanation of true self entirely, so I have opted for a brief description of who you truly are.

We often identify with material things – things of this world – and confuse these things with our true selves. To consider yourself your job, hobbies, interests, religion, political stance, intelligence, skills, friends, relationships, or physical attributes as who you truly are is to miss the source of it all. If any of these were to change, your true self does not change. This is a difficult concept to grasp early on. Once you find and experience yourself as that which gives you life, which gives everything life, the worldly identifiers listed above seem to be desperate attempts to differentiate us from one another, and nothing more. In fact, the truest self we have is shared with all other beings. Worldly attributes, by way of ego, differentiate and separate, while our being brings us together. Before we can attempt to define and find the true self, what is not self must be learned.

We all have egos. Our egos judge, others and ourselves. It clings to the past and future, constantly regretting things that happened, and fearing things to come. It is obsessed with what others think of you. The great realization to finding your true self is this: You are not your ego. Nay, your ego is but a small portion of your entire being. We learn from a young age to rely on our egos for survival, but it grows like a fungus, and invades our being to the point that we forget the amazing people we truly are at the core. Our egos love the worldly attributes that separate, thus giving it its identity and reason to be.

We are not our egos, but who are we, really? Our true self is permanent. It's the only part of us that is permanent. Beyond our egos lie our true selves. With practice, we can filter out everything our ego throws at us in its constant attempt to rule our lives, and what remains beyond ego is the self.

For instance, we think we are our thoughts, but if we stop thinking, do we cease to exist? We suspect we are our bodies, but if we lose an arm, do we cease to exist fully? There is something inside us beyond our physicality. Find it, and find truth.

You could never take my word for it, nor do I ask you to. Finding your true self is far beyond any quip or quote I can offer. The only way to discover your true self is to experience it on your own. You must experience it to appreciate it. We experience life through our minds every day. The challenge I present is to experience life, but not through the mind. Mysterious, I know. "Is he speaking in metaphors?" You will know when you have the answer.

Meditate. You sit, and you learn to quiet the mind. Experience what goes on within you, including heartbeats, physical receptors, emotions, thoughts, and... what else? There is a part of us beyond all of these things that cannot be explained in words. Such is the difficulty in describing to another your true self. Meditation is not a trance, but enhanced awareness. During this self-examination, judge nothing that happens within you. There is no judgment without the ego, and by judging your thoughts, you feed the ego. Your goal is to experience yourself, but not through the mind. Observe your mind from outside the mind. Eventually, your mind calms, and all that remains is you. You are there, pure and complete. No mind, no ego, just you. You are aware, and you are conscious. This awareness and consciousness is the true you. You contain within you a slice of God (or whatever you want to call it that gives you life), and it is the same "life" that is within all living things. We are all one.

No religion is necessary. The only dogmatic principal necessary is to believe that "I am more than my physical body." Even then, you only have to have faith in this statement temporarily until you find it on your own and experience it.

To embark on any journey, you must want it, you must believe you are capable of it, and you must believe you deserve it. Capability and worthiness are built into us all. They are inalienable rights inherent in the very thing that gives us life. As for wanting it, if you glimpsed a sliver of the success that awaits you once you've acquired internal self-worth, you'd want it.

For, once you've found your true self, you will begin to see the world for what it is, like a flower blossoming as you've never seen before. That you are a direct expression of God will be so obvious, and to be any level of imposter will seem preposterous. You see that you do not need the possessions, relationships, skillsets, and opinions that you have, up to this point, viewed as your identity. You are far more than that, and these worldly novelties are fleeting. From this point on, all interactions will be sweeter, every day will be brighter, and every breath will feel like pure love filling your being to the brim.

That is the best I can do in explaining how to find your true self while keeping it brief. Please, if you have not done so already, read the books that led me on this journey, and live the life you truly deserve. I assure you, it is worth the effort. No faith is necessary, except perhaps a small bit of temporary faith. You must have at least enough faith to look into yourself to see if you exist beyond the mind. Seek, and ye shall find, and I mean this in its most literal sense. If you can truly silence the mind (yet not by force), recognize all forms of ego for what it is, and you cease to exist, then send me an "I told you so" letter. If, however, you like what you find, then faith is no longer necessary because you have experienced it firsthand, and your faith has transformed to knowledge.

Finding yourself is the cure-all - the one thing that truly makes all other problems dissolve. This should be your main focus, but it is not something that will happen overnight. Learning to recognize the ego is a process.

While you focus on self-discovery, life continues to happen all around you. I won't disappoint. Again, I have not mentioned diapers in many pages, and this is a book about Adult Babies, isn't it? Fear not, for I offer more direct insight into the specific problems Adult

Babies face in their lives. Perhaps it will offer more insight into your true self, and how to love that self, as well.

SHOULD YOU STOP WEARING DIAPERS?

Being Adult Babies, we face social problems. What if someone sees my diapers? How will I tell my girlfriend? She'll find out eventually, anyway. What happens then? The easiest solution, quite obviously, is to stop wearing diapers and act your age.

Because being an Adult Baby and wearing diapers is so rare in our society, it is looked upon as crazy. People tend to fear what they are not familiar with. As such, we are sure to face a higher frequency of rejection than the average person.

Everyone struggles with his or her identity. Our egos cling to things that don't really matter and make it a part of "who we are". If you're a chocoholic, do you lose your identity if you develop a chocolate allergy? It may seem so on the surface, but it is a mirage. The reality is we remain who we are as things of this world come and go from our lives. All things of this world are temporary, yet your truest self is permanent.

Knowing this, it is important to not identify too deeply with your babyhood. It is one of a million traits that make you who you are. The diaper on your bum becomes artificially inflated as a part of your identity because it is the strangest, most "abnormal", and most likely rejected trait of yours. It's a natural tendency, mind you, but an illusion nonetheless.

Can you stop wearing diapers? The thought may be terrifying. This is the sort of thing that I cannot answer for you. It is true that you are more than an Adult Baby. If you were to quit diapers, you remain the same beautiful, worthy person you were before. Bottom line, it's a choice. It's a simple measure of payoffs.

You get to wear diapers forever, or you avoid some touchy social situations in the future. What is more important to you?

For me, the choice was obvious from the beginning, yet I struggled. I did not want to stop wearing diapers. I loved diapers. If I were to quit diapers altogether, I would miss the feelings they gave me.

Why would I quit? So that others would judge me less? So I wouldn't have to explain my oddity? To me, these seemed like terrible reasons to change my being. While I would enjoy simpler social relations, I would be quitting for other judgmental people, not for myself. Also, diapers were a deep part of me, and I would rather struggle through a lifetime of social awkwardness than struggle through a lifetime without diapers.

This is not something I'm bragging about. I consider it a weakness, in fact. I am bothered that diapers have such a grip on me. I would prefer to be in control of my life, rather than the diapers controlling me. To need something so material to this extent is not ideal, and will most certainly cause troubles in the future.

To change your being so that others will look on you more fondly, however, is also far from ideal.

Therefore, it becomes a choice that you will make. I will say that the easiest solution is to stop wearing diapers and stop being an Adult Baby. But it's not always so easy, is it?

We've all tried to stop before, yet the actions continue. The pull is too strong. The desire to wear diapers is so deeply ingrained in us we could not possibly decide not to wear diapers. It's who we are. It's a fact. Right?

Often, the conversations we have with ourselves hold within them their own self-defeating principles. For instance, let us refrain from saying things like "wearing diapers is *who I am*." It's closing us off to any opportunity of change and growth. If we've already decided that wearing diapers is who we are, quitting diapers is out of the question. On the other hand, if we consider wearing diapers a hobby, or a trait, the option to quit is available without losing our identity.

Can we have it both ways? Can we accomplish the idealism of ridding ourselves of the need of diapers, while not quitting for the sake of others? There does exist a solution in which we quit, but for all the right reasons.

The best exercise we can… um… exercise, is to practice living without diapers, allowing ourselves to feel what we feel, and becoming comfortable with those feelings. After we are comfortable non-diapered, we are better suited to make life decisions about diapers. To use Dr. Rush's words, make it a non-angst decision, rather than an ego-based decision. To put another way, make it a conscious decision to wear diapers for pleasure, rather than giving into an attachment, addiction, or pull that forces you to wear them. This is the ultimate challenge for the hardest core Adult Babies, but also, perhaps, holds the greatest reward. One can only endure this process willingly. Nobody can force you through this process, and you cannot force anyone else through this process.

The process described is not about continuing to wear diapers or quitting. It's about ridding yourself of the control that any "thing" has over you and your being. It's about reminding ourselves that diapers are not a need, as we often convince ourselves they are. Ultimately, it's about finding our true selves, and learning the true role that diapers play in our lives, and as such, taking back the control.

We are amazing people. We are all capable of things far beyond what we have ever dreamed of! We should not be so definitive in our actions. Allow yourself the room to adjust and grow. If you decide to stop wearing diapers, do it because you want to, or because it is best for you, not because someone else wants you to.

*   *   *

Many of us carry guilt associated with our actions. We get home after work and first thing we do is put on a nice, thick diaper, preferably with childish prints. Our parents won't approve, our lovers won't approve, our friends won't approve, and God won't approve. We're misfits!

Approval from other people is meaningless. Other people are but mere humans with irrational human biases. Not one of the people is God, and it's reasonable to expect them to be wrong about some things.

Therefore, the only logical conclusion is to develop your own moral code to live by, disregarding what anybody else thinks is right and wrong. You can and should consider what they say, and adjust your code as you see fit, but ultimately, it is up to you to decide how to live your own life. You are who you are, and should not live by anyone's standards but your own. To live by another's standards is to value who *they* think you *should* be over your true self.

Even your moral code should be a living, evolving thing. If you get too closely attached to your code and make it part of your identity, then your ego will refuse to change the code, lest you lose your very self. Your moral code is an opinion, and as such, is fallible. So, while it is the code by which you should live your life, be prepared to adjust it when necessary, for if there are no adjustments, there can be no growth.

Wearing diapers is harmless. The only reason you will face judgment is that it is different, and people fear what is different. No matter which way you slice it, a diaper is harmless. No guilt is legitimized. We should feel guilt when we do something wrong, not when we do something different.

It's interesting how our minds make this connection, isn't it? One theory suggests that "fitting in" was necessary for survival in early humanity. If one were to be rejected from the tribe, he faces starvation and death from the elements. To be rejected is to face death, so it's not surprising that we feel bad feelings when we face judgment, or engage in actions, like wearing a diaper, that may induce rejection. In our modern era, however, there is no need whatsoever for guilt in wearing diapers, no matter what anyone else tells you.

Unless God directly tells you it's wrong. That would be different. Unless God parted the clouds, came down to Earth, and told you directly it's wrong, you are getting that information second hand, through an imperfect and egoistical (as all humans are) person who may not be able to tell the difference between his own standards and God's. If you have religious guilt for wearing diapers, you are being manipulated by other people who want to control you to live by *their* standards - not God's - instead of your own. There is no Biblical basis for claiming that wearing diapers is evil. My parents told me it was evil throughout my childhood, but I can see now that was a human control tactic. There was nothing divine about their claims.

There is something divine about me, though. You are a product of God. I am a product of God. God made me exactly who I am for a purpose. And I enjoy a thick diaper. Therefore, God accepts me and loves me as His creation, diapers and all.

God does not hate you for wearing diapers, nor is He disappointed in you. On the contrary, God loves you for who you are. To have that backward is to be victim of mere humans' desires to control you, and perhaps a victim of your ego's need for the approval of others. True happiness comes from the approval of self.

Being different is not wrong. We are all different. We view diapers as *more* different because of the rejection we face, but this does not make it any more different than anything else. Its bloated significance is an illusion, built on human bias. What is not illusion is your being. You are, in fact, who you are. Resist if you want, but no good will come of it. Accept reality, and watch your life improve.

We can boil this issue down to acceptance and resistance. But what do we accept? What do we resist?

Do we accept that diapers are not such a big part of us after all? Or do we accept that wearing diapers is perfectly acceptable, and that any reason not to stems from hollow social acceptance?

Look, I never said this was simple. You were expecting maybe a "yes" or a "no." The answer lies within you. Maybe you already know. Look into yourself, find the reasons you do what you do, and decide for yourself if they are good reasons or bad. How important to you is wearing diapers?

I can confidently say that the choice to stop wearing diapers, if your being will allow it, is the best choice to make. Life is easier, you are happier, you have one less worldly fixation, more options for relationships, no diaper rash, and the list goes on. Not all of our inner beings will allow it, though, and therein lies the necessity for the rest of this book.

ARE YOU AN ADULT BABY?

How important to you is wearing diapers? Do you merely dabble in diapers? I mean, can you go months or years without them, and then, one day at a fetish party, put them on and dance around, and label yourself a Diaper Lover?

I'm not saying you're *not* a Diaper Lover. It just might not be such a big deal to you. You may be reading this book and asking yourself why I'm making such a big deal over such a little fetish?

As with any interest, there exists a wide range of enthusiasts. Some dabble, some dive in. Some people wear a diaper once a year, or maybe they never do and just like the idea. Some live their entire adult lives in diapers, onesies, high chairs and cribs, forever rejecting adulthood.

The importance of babyhood also varies. One enjoys it, but could easily go his entire life without it and not think twice. Another may go a day or two without diapers and lose sleep over the discomfort.

Much of this advice applies only to the folks at the steeper end of the spectrum. If you can go the entirety of your life without ever indulging in diapers and Adult Babyhood, then why would you expose your relationships to the following hardships? The risk may not be worth the reward.

If you are an Adult Baby, and could not imagine being anything but, these following lessons will be entirely helpful.

How do you know which camp you're in? Only you can decide. Again, I revisit your happiness level. If you're fulfilled, why change? If you are unhappy, something's got to change. Who you are is something you must discover for yourself.

But let's say that you are an Adult Baby. What does that even mean? That you like to wear diapers?

That you act like a baby? You like bottles? Baby food? Pacifiers? Baby talk?

It is easy to fall into roles. For instance, at age fifteen I liked to wear diapers. I found others online who shared my interest in diapers, and they were Adult Babies who enjoyed baby talk and footies and onesies. I concluded that I, too, must like baby talk and footies and onesies. I was too young to recognize my individuality outside of a role. For the first time in my life, I found a group of other people that liked diapers into which I was welcomed, and I immersed myself in the group. I was into diapers far more than bottles, but when in Rome…

It is important that we not fall into the role of being an Adult Baby. Just be yourself, and be proud of who you are. Do what you enjoy. What others think of you, in or out of the AB community, is meaningless.

That's not to say there is no value in branching out and trying new things. You must find the line between experimenting in order to expand your world and doing things you are uncomfortable doing. In other words, expand your lines, but don't cross them.

You are who you are. Forget the term Adult Baby. You are you, and you like what you like. Other people brand you an Adult Baby because it is easier for them to understand you. We may even brand ourselves Adult Babies because it is then easier for us to understand ourselves. Our egos love labels to help us understand the world in strictly defined terms. In real life we are undefined. We are works of art, and no label could possibly capture, or rightly define, our entire being.

The majority of judgment directed my way, ironically, is from within the AB community! I am confident this results from people's lack of confidence in who they are. They feel different, like a freak. By labelling you different or a freak, they make themselves feel better about who they are. It's an empty boost, and will never last. It never ceases to amaze me how a group of people gathered together *because* of a common major difference are so quick to judge within the group for their minor differences.

Babies like me who strive for the freedom of being public are hated - literally *hated* - from within the community. There is no valid reason for this, although I tend to believe there is never a valid reason for hatred. The only explanation is these people are so insecure with themselves that they channel that insecurity outward. Their belief is that if I were to come out, it would reflect poorly on them.

The worst part of this is that it hampers the advancement of the Adult Baby community. How will we ever get the rest of the world to accept us as valuable members of society if we continue bickering amongst ourselves from within the group? It's ridiculous.

The answer is simple. Once you accept yourself for who you are meant to be, the next logical step is to accept other people for who they are meant to be. It is the same life force that flows within us all.

So do what you are comfortable doing as if nobody was watching. You are not a role, you are you. Adult Baby is a blanket term to help others categorize you, and should mean nothing to you about who you truly are. Practice not caring what others think of your actions. It's difficult at first, but gets easier over time. Remind yourself that they are not God, and you needn't live by their standards. You decide what is right for you. It is somewhat easy to know what is right for you, because the answer is within you.

DIAPERED IN PUBLIC

Should you wear diapers in public? (I'm talking under your clothes) Finally, I have a simple answer: If you want to.

Some people are uncomfortable being diapered in public. They are far too concerned with what would happen if they were "caught."

I wear diapers 24/7. I was caught once - yes, only once - and it was about as eventful as Y2K. I was at work walking to the break room. Behind me, two coworkers, a man and woman, were following me. The guy chimed in, "Brian, are you wearing a diaper?"

I looked at him funny, and said "yeah, thanks." The look told him that his question was very inappropriate, which it was. The girl proceeded to slap him, which I got a kick out of. I never, ever heard anything about it since. Sorry that wasn't the epic story you've created in your mind about what will happen when you will be "caught."

My choice was clear. I want to wear diapers all the time, and I want to care not for others' opinions, so I wear diapers all the time. However, part of knowing yourself is knowing when you are uncomfortable about something. If you are uncomfortable because you feel you lack the freedom to wear diapers around the town, then a change is in order, and you should expand your comfort lines in attempt to wear more often. Start with a trip to the gas station, then the library, and soon you will realize that nobody notices or cares what you wear beneath your pants. I advise you to practice, little by little, not caring what others think about you.

If, however, you are content keeping diapers in the privacy of your home, have no urge to wear them out, and are far more discomforted by the thought of wearing them publicly, then why in the world would you? No brainer.

It is odd, I know, that I suggest here that you practice to wear diapers, and earlier I suggest that you practice to not. I am attempting to address all issues Adult Babies may face. I doubt that, in your current life situation, you need to practice wearing diapers *and* going without diapers, but I am sure that many of the readers are in one or the other situation. Define your life goals and act accordingly. I want you to be free, to have the ability to be yourself, but I also do not want your life controlled by diapers.

CRAVING EXPOSURE

If your desires to be diapered, combined with your desires to be loved and accepted, are suppressed for long enough, you may find yourself craving to be seen. The context of this exposure does not seem so important as our desperation to be seen takes over. This is more common than you'd think. Recall my experience at the movie theater from Section 2. Don't fall into these habits.

Be yourself, and be free, but do it for the right reasons. Be yourself for the sake of being yourself. Being proud of who you are is different than bragging about or showing off who you are.

The desire to go out in public wearing only a diaper may be strong, but the drives may not be healthy. More than likely, you are attempting to fulfill needs that are widely available to you without the risks that wearing a diaper in public present. You want to be seen and accepted, but ultimately, you want what benefits you the most.

To be clear, I find nothing morally wrong with walking around in only a diaper. I am not a good representative of the world, though. I believe that you would offend other people, you risk being attacked, and you risk criminal charges. You most certainly will not be looked upon in a good light.

While what others think of you should not be the driving force behind your decisions, there may be better options available to you. For instance, forming meaningful relationships in which you are your true self, and you needn't hide the fact that you are diapered and babied, can fulfill the desire to be seen and accepted. Finding other fetishists with similar interests could fulfill your need to be diapered openly.

Consider nudists, who are also unable to freely be themselves without legal exposure, no pun intended. Personally, I do not believe it's right, but it is the way of the world. Our goals should be focused on giving ourselves the best lives possible, while working within our circle of influence. Going out in short-alls fulfills my need to be babied in the world and be myself and proud of it, while limiting my risk of prosecution. Dancing in the street wearing only a diaper does not fulfill my needs any better, yet increases my risk, thus defeating the goal of bettering my life.

Finding the balance is one of the great challenges of life. Be yourself while following the rules of the world, while not always possible, can be balanced. It is up to you to decide whose rules you will bend to better suit your needs. Self-awareness is the key. Why we do things, and want to do things, hold the answers to these problems. Invest in this self-discovery, and these challenges of fitting into society will become much easier knowing exactly whose rules (yours or theirs) to bend and when.

The sooner we release these suppressed desires, the less likely they will manifest in an unhealthy manner.

*   *   *

Reading on, I address situations that are more specific. Generally, it is for Adult Babies who have decided to continue the lifestyle, accepted it as a part of who they are, and are unsatisfied with their social life as it currently is. Only you can determine if each section applies to you personally.

WHEN TO TELL OTHERS

You've lived your entire life with a secret. You love the feeling of a diaper wrapped around your waist. You sneak them when nobody's around. You indulge at every glimpse of privacy, but never have you even dreamt of telling someone close to you. You've wanted to, but you've been scared.

It's ok to be scared. We are human, and humans fear rejection. The most successful of us don't avoid rejection, but cherish it as a necessary step to a truly fulfilling life. Of course, this practice takes... um... practice.

We must accept that if they reject us, it does not mean we are bad people. Rejection tells us more about their biases than our own validity in this world.

Still, it's tough. When is the right time? What is the right way? What should I expect?

No matter who you plan to tell, there is a right time and a wrong time to tell them you are an Adult Baby. The wrong time is before you've come to terms with who you are. The right time is after your self-worth comes from within.

It becomes a bad habit to tell people for the wrong reasons. The wrong reasons, in a nutshell, are to receive acceptance, love, or other desirable attention in return.

But wait, it's not that simple. It is true that by telling your loved ones, you open yourself up to the greatest love and acceptance available on Earth. This is not a bad goal to have. So where's the line?

The line is based on how conditional the hearer's response is. It comes down to your expectations. For instance, I tell my new girlfriend I have a thing for diapers. What am I expecting?

Consider a scenario of two fictional characters named Henry and Steve. If Henry is looking for some type of acceptance to give him a sense of internal belonging, that would be a bad reason to tell his girlfriend. Put another way, if you are looking for a type of validation, forget it. You are not ready to tell anyone.

Steve, however, has no expectations, and sees the situation as a simple trade off. Either his girlfriend takes it well and the relationship will be all the better, or she freaks out and leaves, thus freeing him from a doomed relationship! Steve has found himself in a win-win situation because his self-worth comes from within.

Henry, meanwhile, is in a win-lose situation. She accepts him and he's ecstatic, or she rejects him, and he's devastated. What's worse is that Henry's win is temporary, as his happiness is dependent upon his love interest's acceptance of him.

Picture a relationship like a bridge; you on one end, and your lover on the other. The relationship (bridge) itself relies on the solid foundation of each end.

In Henry's case, his end's foundation is supported only by the other end, and the bridge is sure to tumble. Worse, when the bridge tumbles, Henry tumbles with it.

Steve has a solid foundation within himself. The bridge is more likely to sustain, but even if the bridge tumbles, Steve will stand strong.

The difference between the right and wrong time to tell is the state of mind. Is a positive outcome dependent on the person's reaction? If so, you have some internal growing to do. I do not recommend you telling *anyone*.

If you will find yourself freer after you tell this person, regardless of the person's reaction, you are ready, Daniel-san.

Finding yourself in a relationship in which you are unable to be yourself begs the question: what the heck are you doing in that relationship anyway? You must be attached to that relationship in some egoistic sense if you are unwilling to attempt to strengthen it. Textbook dependency. That's the catch. You must risk it to strengthen it. It's a gamble, but with little to lose and much to gain.

What you have to lose is the illusion of a real relationship. What you have to gain is the healthiest, truest, richest relationship you could imagine having with a person.

We must accept that if they reject us, it does not mean we are bad people. It simply shows us their biases.

TELLING YOUR PARENTS

With family, it is more difficult. In a sense, it is more necessary to tell your family, and you should be your true self among them before any other. In another, if feels like you have far more to lose in family than with outsiders. Thus, the drive to preserve the relationship is strong.

Unfortunately, many of us have self-doubt, and trouble with deciphering who we really are. This is often a result of parents who've unconsciously *required* us to create a character in order to be loved, as their love didn't feel unconditional. If their love appears conditional, showing our true selves to family is an intimidating and daunting task.

There are two situations in which you'd tell your parents. Either you're a minor still living at home, or you are already an adult.

If an adult tells his family, and they disown him, his life continues. Ideally, he had a rich life with his own self-worth before the confession, and his family's rejection didn't affect him to the point his life is ruined. If, on the other hand, a fifteen year old tells his parents and they disown him, he is doomed.

For adults, do what you feel is right. Do not let fear drive your actions. Often, fear is a sign we're on the right path. If anything, we should face the fear, do what we fear, and grow. If you are not comfortable telling your parents, *and* you are content keeping it hidden, then do not tell them. Why would you? You're already happy, right? If you feel like nothing is wrong, then you have no reason to change.

But maybe you feel like you've never given your parents the chance to accept you for who you are. You are robbing yourself of the unconditional love only a parent can provide, but you are also robbing your parents of the opportunity to accept you for who you are. Wouldn't you want to know your child inside and out so you could love him as he is?

I remember the day I realized I rejected myself for people so they didn't have to. *Why would I ask this girl out? She'll just say no.* I get all the negative feelings of rejection without the opportunity for success! The rejection was but a figment of my imagination. Learn from my mistakes. Give people the chance to accept or reject you. Do not make the decision for them.

Even with parents, we must risk it to improve it. The act of telling your parents you are an Adult Baby still cannot be hinged on the results. As an adult, you are no longer in need of your parents to provide. Growing up, your relationship with your parents has gradually transformed into a voluntary one, which you choose to continue based on its richness. They know you better than anyone, or at least they should.

So the questions become: Do you want a richer relationship with your parents, including the ability to be your true self, and the unconditional love that comes with it? And are you willing to risk what you have now to get it?

Rejection is plausible! I will not tell you it won't hurt. Yet, it is necessary. You owe it to yourself to live your life as you. If they reject you, it does not say anything about you, who you are, or your worthiness in this world. As a child, your parents were like gods, providers of sustenance, commanders of expectations, and protectors of children. As an adult, your parents are just other adults with their own faults and biases. There is no greater tragedy to me than a parent rejecting their kin for being who they are, but it happens every day to no fault of the children.

Yet, it's difficult for me to put too much blame on the parents. Parents, being imperfect people, often get stuck in co-dependent cycles themselves, inadvertently causing emotional damage to their children without the slightest bit of awareness of what they are doing. They may, on some level, know that something isn't right, but having never known any alternative, continue the cycles indefinitely.

Parents are people, and people can be insecure.

*   *   *

As a minor, things are different. You rely on your parents for survival, making the situation a little stickier. A parent/minor relationship, unlike a parent/adult-child relationship, is mandatory, so the complications abound. Many things should be considered.

First, are you a practicing ABDL? Do you keep diapers in the house? If so, you run the risk of being "caught" by your parents, a far more pivotal event than being caught by a peer. This must be considered in your evaluation. Things are likely to be worse being caught than if you openly confessed.

Second, how accepting are your parents? Do they expect you to be something they want, or do they allow you the freedom to express yourself and be your own person? Are they the "my house/my rules" type of parents? Will they love you no matter what? Do not judge your parents for whatever they are. They are imperfect people trying their best. Still, considering the answers to these questions is important to making your decision.

Third, how important is it to you? Don't compare yourself to the others in the online groups. Ask yourself, honestly, is it a fantasy, a fetish, or something that is truly a deeper part of you? If it's just a fetish, it might be private. If it's a fantasy you can live without, then live without it until your life situation can adapt. If you cannot live without it, factor this into making your decision. I, at age fifteen, could not live without it. But I'm me, and you're you. Do not make your decision based on my being.

Determining how important anything is to you proves difficult as a youth without the experience of life. Youths inflate some things that don't matter, and ignore other things that matter immensely. Just do your best. Spend time thinking about who you really are and why you do things. This is not a decision to be rushed.

If you have parents that are not understanding, expect you to live by their standards, don't allow you to be different, and are abusive, while you don't wear diapers currently and could easily go your entire life without them, then clearly you should not tell your parents.

If your parents are understanding, allow you to be your own person, won't abuse you, and you don't feel like you could go another day without a diaper, you may be a candidate to tell your parents the truth. "I'm not sure how to tell you this, but I find myself with extremely strong and strange impulses to wear diapers. I'm not sure why, and I could really use some help understanding these desires." Honesty is key, and if they start yelling, explain to them how they are making it uncomfortable for you to be truthful with them. Perhaps this book's Section 4 would help ease their discomfort on the subject. Until now, as far as I know, there is no other book like it. If you tell and things go poorly, hand it over for them to read.

Evaluate the situation and weigh your options.

Yet still, you have to make the decision. It's worth repeating: If you're unhappy, something must change. If you are truly happy inside, then change is not necessary, nor is risking your relationships.

There are two basic scenarios that result from a minor telling his parents, with one variation. First, they could accept you and love you for who you are. Your relationship with your parents will never have been stronger, and their and your lives will be far richer forever and ever.

Second possible result, they become very angry and upset. It would hurt, but ultimately, you didn't really choose who you are. You are who you are. You are an expression of God. That other people don't like that or don't agree with it is moot. Be proud of who you are. Your parents are just people, and they don't know everything. They don't yet understand that you are as the universe made you because they still believe that you are as they made you, and this is not what they planned. Most likely, they haven't learned to love themselves. They feel like they messed up in raising you, and that you can change if you tried hard enough. Kids often get the brunt of parents' insecurities. You are not insane for wanting to wear diapers.

If you now feel worthless, guilty and self-hating because your parents do not accept you for who you are, then you were not ready to tell them in the first place. While these feelings will be inevitably conjured when facing rejection, they do not drastically affect the mentally prepared. The only valid love, acceptance, and worthiness will come from within you. In the event you already came clean before you loved yourself, the solution to your new problem is – you guessed it - to learn to love yourself.

The alternative situation is that they neither accept nor reject the situation, but deny it. They'll brush it off and insist it's a phase or whatever, and pretend like it didn't happen. Again, Section 4 may help. I am hoping that hearing my story, a healthy Adult Baby with a great life, will cure their uneasiness and fear and give insight into what you may be dealing with. While the life of an Adult Baby is not an easy one, discovering your children are Adult Babies is difficult as well. Let's respect that. Parents want what's best for their children, and can't foresee a healthy lifestyle that includes diapers. What they fail to realize is that parental rejection will undoubtedly cause far more pain than wearing diapers.

If they are in denial, reassess. Is it worth pressing? If you tell them it's not a phase, but ingrained in your being, will they freak out and react angrily, or will they eventually come to accept it? The denial itself suggests rejection, but you never know. Sometimes denial is easier than going through the difficult process of accepting something strange to them as their own loved one.

If rejection is certain, then I actually condone lying. Please understand that this is not ideal, and should not be used as the easy way out when faced with the difficulty of telling them the truth. The right thing to do is to tell the truth, damn the consequences, because you are you, and others' rejection should not affect the way you live your life. Being afraid is natural, and not a good reason to lie. The exception is if you are a prisoner, as is the case of a minor to one's parents, where the minor must maintain a relationship beyond the potential rejection, and said continued relationship is abusive. Still, I'd like to see a child or teen tell their parents the truth, and in turn, I'd like to see the parents accept the minor for who they are. However, the reality is that there are many minors in unhealthy homes with unhealthy parents. I would hate to see them tell the truth and be treated terribly for it (even still, no blame could be placed on the children for being themselves). If this abuse is inevitable, then lie. Tell your parents you wet the bed, or wet your pants, and you don't know what's wrong. This way, you can get the diapers you so desperately need, without the hateful judgment in your direction. These unloving parents are likely to be happier being lied to, in ignorant bliss, tending to their child's special needs as opposed to dealing with what would be considered perversion.

But wait! Some of the worst parents would treat their children poorly even for having a bladder control problem! Even a medical condition of their child could reflect poorly on them in their eyes, and if the parents are that insecure with themselves, they will undoubtedly take it out on their child. Even if you do lie, and they buy it, it could still have awful consequences. They may not get you treatment. Or they may get you the treatment, and diapers, but continue to ridicule and belittle you along the way. Some situations are unwinnable. I am afraid that if your parents are that far gone, Section 4 may not be of any help to you - or rather - them.

I would like to believe that the strong majority of parents at least want their children to have good lives. I would hope that the scenario I have just described is an extremely rare one.

(A quick note to all the parents that are shocked and appalled that I dare suggest their children lie to you. If you are accepting and loving of your children, and they know it, then I'm not talking to your children, and you have nothing to worry about. If you think that your child is terrible because he enjoys the comfort of wearing diapers, and you will treat him as such, I stand by my suggestion to lie to you. To these parents, you should read the section about finding your true self, entitled The Basics, that you might realize your child's being in no way reflects poorly on your own.)

Please understand. Lying is a last resort, only to be used in the worst of circumstances. In most cases, the truth is the far better option. I fear that by condoning lying in these rare circumstances, some minors will misread their own situations and lie to non-abusive parents. I think about my own childhood and teen years, and I truly think my parents and I all would have been better off had I told the lie, and I would have a hard time feeling guilty about it now. I value honesty above nearly everything else, but it is important to remember that a parent/minor relationship is obligatory, which changes things a bit.

Even in the case of a minor, self-acceptance must come first. Do not tell your parents before you are prepared internally. Learn to love yourself despite what even your parents think of you. To live by another's standards is to value who *they* think you *should* be over your true self. This is true even with parents. You are who you are.

*   *   *

To summarize the parent/child relationship (including adult-children): As young children, we need love from our parents. If we do not have the ability to express ourselves and be loved as we are, we take on a role that *is* loved to fulfill the need to be loved, and our true selves become repressed. For these children entering adulthood, both the role we've created and the repressed frustration continue, causing increasing emotional pain that we can't understand, mostly because we don't realize or refuse to admit that we're playing a character. After some time, the pain gets so intense that we seek answers as to why we feel pain, and are then able to kill off the character and be our true selves. Often, we become parents before we reach that level of pain, and our children follow the character creating pattern to live up to *our* expectations to fulfill their own needs. Parents fill a role, and expect their children to fill a role, all without being aware of what they are doing or why. Often, the only sign is a general uneasiness, social nervousness, or vague internal unhappiness. If a parent has never known unconditional love, how could he possibly provide it?

Any individual can break this cycle by looking inward and finding his true self. You are not responsible for being in such a situation, but you are responsible for getting out of it.

TELLING YOUR LOVER

With your boyfriend, your girlfriend, your significant other, or your love interest, the option to lie is gone. You are not shackled to this relationship; therefore, you must be yourself. You're an adult now, and you do not need anyone else for your happiness. If you do rely on others for your inner happiness, you are not ready to make the decision whether to tell your lover that you are a toddler at heart. As with all relationships, finding your true self must come first.

Assuming you want the best life achievable, including the strongest relationships achievable, you *must* tell your lover of your true nature. As was the case with Henry and Steve, you must be sure of yourself before you can branch out to others.

If you have a solid foundation built from within, you will be facing a win-win situation. If you are rejected, you have ridden yourself of the shallow relationship, thus opening opportunities for a better one.

A lover can reject you for any number of reasons, hair color, weight, bad jokes (that one happened to me countless times!), whatever. If you tell her you wear diapers and she rejects you for that, it holds no more weight than rejection over any other trait she is uncomfortable with. It does not say anything about you. It is only telling of her own biases.

The choice is yours. Continue the façade, or gamble with the truth. In gambling, you risk the false relationship based on lies for a chance to gain the healthiest relationship you've ever imagined. Be truthful and be loved for who you are. Lie and not be loved at all. Your lover will still love "you", if you can call that "you." In reality, it is the disguise you have created that will receive all the love, and your true self will wither. To be loved, you must be yourself.

If your expectation is acceptance, and rejection would cast you to a pit of despair, you, like Henry, are not ready to make this decision. Learn to love yourself first. You are who you are. That is a fact. To reject you is to reject reality. What others think of you does not matter. Your self-worth cannot rely on the opinions of others, or you will never, ever live a fulfilling life.

STARTING NEW RELATIONSHIPS

In building new relationships, Adult Babies struggle with when to disclose this sensitive information.

Say, for instance, you've been into this girl for a week or two, talking, maybe a couple dates, and things are heating up. She has no idea that you're an Adult Baby. How and when do you tell her?

You can't very well start introducing yourself to strangers, "Hi, I'm Brian. I'm an Adult Baby. I'm wearing wet diapers right now, as a matter of fact!" That's weird, and people won't like it, not because you're an Adult Baby, but because you appear to identify solely as an Adult Baby. Wait too long to tell, on the other hand, and you will appear to be a liar, withholding pertinent information about who you are.

A balance must be found. I suggest the point in the relationship that you can make a relatively accurate assumption on the future of the relationship. For instance, if you've been dating for a couple weeks, and you see potential for a relationship here, then it might be time to tell her that you like diapers. Honesty, as always, is the best policy. You must be proud of who you are, and portray yourself as such. And most importantly, be ready to handle rejection. If you will be utterly devastated upon rejection, then you were not ready to tell her, nor were you ready to date. Contrarily, you should be ready to cherish rejection, having dodged the bullet of an unfulfilling relationship with a shallow person.

It helps to think of diapers in its real form, as one of our many traits, rather than its social form, a freak of nature. If we are insecure about ourselves, finding a healthy relationship at all is even tougher than gathering the courage to tell someone about it. If we are telling in order to get acceptance, we are not ready to tell or date. The proper reason to be forthright is the win-win results. We are released from a doomed relationship, or we have opened ourselves up to an amazing one.

This state of mind is easier said than done, but with practice, you will master it, and in doing so, you will master life. Being yourself acts as a filter, sifting out all the people that won't make good friends.

TELLING YOUR FRIENDS

Decide how important this relationship is to you. You may think that the less important it is to you, the easier it is to risk. I would suggest the opposite. If the friendship is important to you, it becomes more necessary to tell them who you really are.

What kinds of friendships do you want? The kinds where you have to censor yourself? The kinds where you portray this imaginary character they are sure to accept in order to keep them around? Or do you want the freedom to be your true self?

When I was in the closet, I felt like I had no true friends. Now that I do have true friends, the previous statement feels all the more true. Some people can live their entire lives without true open friendships. Some people can keep parts of their lives hidden forever and endure nary a drop of dissatisfaction. In a way, I envy these people, as they enjoy inner peace without enduring the vulnerability I experienced in coming out and telling those most important to me of my fondness for diapers and pacifiers. On the other hand, I have some amazing relationships now that I never could have experienced had I been satisfied in disguise.

True friends love you for you. True friends are honest and accepting.

I had none of those friends, but to be fair, Old Brian did not give them the chance. It was agonizing. I felt like I was living a lie. People didn't know the true me. They were friends with this portrayal of me, and if they knew what a freak I was there would be no friendship. I did not like this feeling, yet couldn't tell them at risk of losing the relationship. In hindsight, I relied on the relationship for my own self-worth, which was my cardinal sin. Now I see the greatness I had to gain and the insignificance of what I had to lose. I assumed they would reject me, so I kept my secrets inside. This was unfair to them and myself. By making their decisions, I only bypassed any hopes of acceptance, ensured the feelings of rejection, and doomed myself to wallow in the scenario I had conjured in my head.

Now I tell. I don't hide the fact that I am an Adult Baby. There is a chance of rejection, and it happens often. At least I can deal with *real* rejection, though, and not something I have imagined in my head. The rejection I face does not affect me much, as I love and accept myself, and I do not rely on them as my sources for love and acceptance. The more positive side is that I face acceptance, *real* acceptance, and with it, the freedom to be myself, and I maintain these friendships without the worries that they would abandon me the second they knew I was diapered.

Not all of my friends know, though. There are different types of friendships. Some friendships are meant to be shallow, and telling them would put an unnecessary strain on the interactions, such as a monthly poker night, but it's up to you. Your closest friends must be given the opportunity to accept you for you if you want any close friends at all. (And you do.)

A life wherein the majority of your relationships you censor yourself inevitably results in perpetual struggle. Ask yourself what kind of friendships you want. Then ask yourself if you are willing to risk some weaker friendships to achieve these goals.

Yes, those that don't accept you will drop off the map, but the ones that stay are your true friends, the ones you've wanted to surround yourself with all along! The ones that are meant to surround you, and you are meant to surround! You lose the false relationships, and gain real ones.

As with all scenarios, the choice is yours. To tell or not to tell, that is the question. The answer differs amongst us all. Most often, the answer can be found by examining your own satisfaction (or lack of) in the current situation. If you accept who you are, and you are unhappy with the current situation, change it. If the current situation includes your closest friend not knowing this aspect of you that is so very important to you, a spill of your guts is required.

I could try to express to you the peacefulness that accompanies the freedom to suck pacifiers while at the movies with friends, or the ability to bend over or lift my arms without the fear of being found out when someone catches a glance of the diaper's elastic around my waist, but I could not do it justice. I can point the finger, but you must look at the moon to understand it. Comfort within one's own skin is incomparable.

TELLING YOUR SPOUSE

It is terribly immature, but human nature, to look at marriage as ownership. All too often, people will play the part to lock down the relationship. After the wedding they allow themselves the freedom to be themselves, and their lover is obligated to stay. Nothing kills an imposter like a wedding, I suppose. This is unfair to your lover and to you.

If you find yourself engaged, or are considering proposing, and your lover doesn't know you wear diapers, I beg you to reconsider. It's natural to fear that nobody will ever love you like this person does, but this person does not love you! This person doesn't even know you! You have not given this person the opportunity to love you if you have not been honest with yourself or your lover.

The best way to avoid a situation in which you are married to someone that doesn't love you is to be yourself before the marriage. An ounce of prevention is worth a pound of cure.

Before the commitment, withholding the pertinent information seems like the right thing to do. You love this person, you want to be with this person, but you're still waiting for the right time to come clean. You fear the rejection. How would you explain the sudden break-off of the wedding to your friends and family?

As soon as you're married, though, you realize that you have made a mistake. Now you are stuck in this prison in which you are unable to be yourself, the worst crime to humanity committed by yourself and against yourself.

My best advice is to avoid getting into this situation at all. If you cannot be yourself, then you are not ready for marriage, or any relationship. Self-acceptance is the first goal of your life.

But that doesn't help those that are already in the situation, does it? Maybe you are married now, and you missed the opportunity to be yourself before the wedding! How do you tell your spouse that you are an Adult Baby?

I will assume that, since you're reading this, you are not happy with the situation as it is. There must be some level of frustration inside you that nags at you, "This is not how I want to live." Nobody should live that way, surrounded by people that don't accept them for who they are, constantly in fear of being discovered. I pity imposters for feeling stuck.

First of all, accept the situation. We go through life doing the best we can, but we will all make mistakes. That much is unmistakable. I was in the habit of living for external validation for years without the slightest idea that anything was amiss. It never felt right, but I'd never imagined any other way of living. Forgive yourself. Guilt keeps you focused on past mistakes which are no longer in existence outside of your mind. Get past guilt, and focus on what you can do now to make things better.

Next, accept yourself. To reject yourself is to reject reality. This is true with you, your spouse, and anyone else in the world. Accept the fact- and this is *fact*- that you deserve to be yourself. You are you for a purpose, and it is your duty to be that person. Acceptance from others is irrelevant. People spend their entire lives trying to control others, trying to control what they think. It's absurdity to attempt to control what others think about you! The greatest value you can get from your life is to live it how you want to live.

Then, tell your partner the truth. Be honest. Explain why you haven't told them yet of your desires, and why you're telling them now. There is no need to be defensive. They will accept you, or they will reject you. This is beyond your control. Either way, being true to yourself and honest with the world will always bring you the greater good.

It's entirely possible you will lose the relationship, but remind yourself of the emptiness of the relationship to begin with, and you will not mourn its loss, but rejoice in it. You were never meant to be with that person in the first place if they don't want to be with an Adult Baby. The person that belonged in that situation was the character you've created for yourself. Now you are open to better relationships in which you actually belong. The freedom to be yourself, along with the feeling of true love and acceptance, will far outweigh whatever feelings you get from your current, shallow relationship. Do not fear its loss, embrace it. This relationship was built on lies in the first place. If you are unfulfilled, change is good.

The alternative result is acceptance. This has obvious benefits in which you keep the relationship and vastly improve upon it! The freedom to be yourself, and the feelings of true love and acceptance, will far outweigh whatever risk and vulnerability you endure in coming clean.

Whether your spouse accepts or rejects you, the ultimate result of being truthful is the freedom to be yourself, and the feelings of true love and acceptance. If these are not your goals, put this book down. It's not for you.

*   *   *

What if you are already in a marriage and your spouse is aware of your kinks, but does not want anything to do with them? For starters, ask yourself how happy you are in the situation.

Ideally, you wouldn't be in the situation without making the conscious decision to enter the situation. Healthy, self-respecting adults will be 100% honest about who they are before there is any chance of marriage, giving their partner a chance to truly accept or reject. If I wanted to propose to my girlfriend, and I told her I am an Adult Baby, and she did not want anything to do with it, I could not possibly imagine going on with the relationship. But who am I to say that it would be unfulfilling for someone else? Maybe you can be happy in a relationship with someone who accepts 90% of you, and pretends the rest doesn't exist, but it's hard for me to imagine. I believe acceptance is an all or none definition. The only kind of acceptance is total acceptance.

More likely, you find yourself in the situation because you weren't entirely honest about who you were before the wedding. I believe this pre-wedding dishonesty is the cause of most divorces. Maybe the subject of diapers was brought up, but not *addressed*. Well, there's no time like the present. You've gotten yourself into a miserable situation, and only you can choose to get out of it. Whether by releasing you from the unhealthy relationship, or reforming the relationship into a healthy one, the truth shall set you free.

I find that the more comfortable I am with myself, the more comfortable people surrounding me are with me. There is something to this, but it is partially an illusion. I still face the rejection, but having accepted who I am, the rejection is meaningless to me. The true acceptance, however, is still valuable. We are social beings after all. I would say that it is actually easier to accept someone that accepts himself, but self-accepting people attract more accepting people in general.

My point is that your first goal, as always, should be to find yourself and accept it. If you approach your spouse with an air of confidence, the likelihood of acceptance is increased. Likewise, rejection, although still possible, or maybe even likely, fades as a significant blow to your esteem.

You deserve to be yourself. You are worthy of love and acceptance just the way you are. Now, start living like it! Embrace the fear and remind yourself that you will gain far more than you lose. You lose empty pseudo-relationships, and gain meaningful ones and the ability to freely express yourself. The path could not be clearer.

WHAT ABOUT THE CHILDREN?

There is one last scenario in a marriage I would like to address. What if you have children in the relationship? Then it might be better to stay hidden. Let's continue the façade, for the sake of the children, right?

Reconsider. A happy married couple is important to a family, but the key word is happy. Children pick up on dysfunction more than you may realize. You're setting the example for them not to be themselves and find true love, but to play the part and stay married no matter how unhappy they may be. I believe that you can set no finer example for your children than being yourself and loving yourself for who you are. Self-acceptance is, in my opinion, the most important characteristic children can learn, and if not from parents, then where?

Worst case scenario, your spouse freaks out, labels you a child molester (as many misunderstanding people label Adult Babies), and fights for custody. Unfortunately, in our culture, being an accused sex offender can have similar consequences to actually being one. However, that other people, like your crazy spouse, would do the wrong thing is *not* a valid reason for you to continue doing the wrong thing. In this scenario, you've done your duty in being your true self, and your spouse has judged and lied and resisted reality resulting in a negative outcome. You would be a victim, but at least you'd then be a victim of someone else. The worst thing to be is a victim of yourself, because you're the only person over whom you have any control.

Now, this is not to say, necessarily, that you should wear your baby clothes around your kids. That may be inappropriate. But it may not be. I think it's important for children to see the world for what it is, made up of billions of individuals made up of different traits. The more kids see that everyone is different - a.k.a. reality - the more likely they are to be accepting of others, and more importantly, of themselves.

In the current culture, we shelter our children from reality, and paint for them a fairytale of normal. Do we not see the damage this causes? They grow up, and it's not long before they realize that they don't fit into the painting of reality they've seen, and they feel like they don't belong. This is true for most children whether they have a big difference - like homosexuality, or an obsession with diapers, or a thing for leather - or they are mostly average/normal.

Kids, from a young age, should be cherished, loved, and accepted, and encouraged to be who they feel like they should be on the inside, regardless of what anyone else thinks of it. As adults, we live our lives contradictory of these lessons, setting a very poor example for the following generation. It comes as no surprise to me that the idealism, judgment, and misunderstanding of others, resulting in wars, murders, hatred and violence continues throughout the ages. Someone must break the cycle.

SOCIAL PATTERNS OF ADULT BABIES

Many Adult Babies live in social fear. They worry that their friends might find out they wear diapers, and they envision future relationships as impossible to create.

We can't enjoy our current relationships, and we fear new relationships.

"As soon as they find out I wear diapers," the Adult Baby says to himself, "the chance for a relationship is over." What we'll often do is avoid social contact altogether, thus avoiding any potential for rejection. Inadvertently, we also avoid the chance for new great relationships, so this is not ideal.

Another thing we might do is confess for the wrong reasons. The second we think that this person actually is a compassionate, nonjudgmental, accepting person, we might confide in them our interest in diapers. We are not attempting to be our true selves, nor do we show any level of confidence. What we are doing is building our own foundation on their acceptance of us. For when they do accept us and tell us "that's ok, doesn't bother me," we catch a glimpse of the good life, and imagine a world in which we are able to be our true selves. It's fleeting, of course, and we soon lose interest in the relationship that is built on co-dependency.

It's an unhealthy routine, continuously jumping from person to person, craving any bit of acceptance, addicted to the words "it's ok." Like any addiction, as time goes on, the craving expands, and we need it more often. The people are meaningless to you. We never ask what we can do for them. We are after something from them, and no good can come of it.

The irony is that the world in which we are able to be our true selves is *this* world, today! We simply can't see it yet. The world isn't broken, *we* are!

Often, the illusion of acceptance comes in the form of other Adult Babies, or those that are attracted to Adult Babies. Getting my diaper changed is a form of acceptance, but empty of true value. An offer to change my diaper is, to a co-dependent Adult Baby, equal to the words "It's ok to be who you are." It's heart-warming to hear, but doesn't last because we don't believe the words.

The only way that these cycles can end is to achieve permanence in your own belief that "it's ok to be who you are." You can't get that from any stranger, lover, or friend. The only permanent solution is to learn for yourself that it is ok to be who you are. We seek externally for what lies internally.

It is impossible to be deeply content in life if your self-worth depends on others' approval.

Adult Babies, I believe, are more likely to experience these issues than the average person. We are more "different" and more "abnormal" than others. It is difficult to believe "it's ok to be who I am" when the world is telling me that it is not. We must examine why the world tells us it's not to see the flaw in their reasoning, and we must examine our true being to see the truth that it is not only ok to be who we are, but entirely necessary.

It is far more important to be yourself than to live a non-offensive life. If people are offended by your actions, what they're really offended by is that God made you who you are, which is asinine!

The world is not perfect, though. If you were to walk around wearing only a diaper, it is not unlikely the cops will be called. Whether you break a law or not is moot. What people fear, they attack, and possibly lock up. You must find the balance. Find a way to express yourself. I go out regularly in my short-alls. My diaper can sometimes be seen from the sides. I have never had an issue. To go to the park wearing only a diaper is far more risky. For many, finding a local AB group to join gives people the outlet they need.

Even within the AB communities there are pitfalls to avoid. For example, we may be under the impression that having such a rare quirk in common, like a passion for diapers, would make any two people great friends. Not true. Wearing diapers is one of many traits. Friends must have common interests and values, and still be honest and accepting with you. The rejection we face as Adult Babies causes socio-psychological problems within us, so it makes sense that healthy Adult Babies are hard to find.

That another person wears diapers will not make him instantly relatable. There is nothing wrong with that. It is the way of the world. Fact: some people will like you, some people will not. Just like you like some people, and not others. Relationships are bonded when you find someone you like that also likes you. Be ready to face rejection, even within the AB community! No need to get discouraged, and certainly no need to create a character. You do need to be willing to face rejection, possibly many times, before reaching the great relationships you seek.

Often, getting involved in AB groups is what we need to find that certain type of friend. I've spoken with many people who don't feel comfortable going out in baby clothes, but feed the need to express themselves at AB parties and munches and the like. I find nothing wrong with this, just limiting. The world is your oyster. I see no reason to restrain your true being to a subculture when, in reality, you will belong just as well in culture. Admittedly, in public culture, you will face rejection from others, but that does not mean you don't belong. It seems to me that these folks get the acceptance from others they need, and the freedom to express themselves, while limiting potential rejection.

I'm not saying it's wrong. AB communities have their place. This serves a great purpose for Adult Babies everywhere to get a sense of belonging. If there are Adult Babies truly content with living in secrecy and only truly living in subgroups, who am I to argue? AB groups, online AB communities, and local AB parties and gatherings may be a great place for you to get your feet wet.

For me, I refuse to limit myself to a subculture. Upon searching inside for my true being, I came upon my purpose. I'm not sure exactly what it is, but I am sure that I am meant to live my life, every day and all day, as who I was created to be. In other words, a life as true self is better than life as an imposter. And for a life in which part of the day is spent as an imposter and another part as the true self? Well, it is an improvement on the full time imposter, yet not quite the full time self.

Looking at the bigger picture, I see long-term social damage by staying hidden. First, society looks at Adult Babies as creepy because it's so rare, yet it's looked upon as so rare because Adult Babies stay hidden. By remaining "discreet", as Adult Babies insist we do, we are sending the message to the world that we are ashamed of who we are and what we do, and that there's something wrong with it. As a group, we can blame nobody for our negative social image but ourselves.

Second, we are doing a disservice to all other Adult Babies. We send the message to the ABDL community that there is something wrong with what we do, and it must be kept hidden. When I was young, I thought I was the only person in the world that wanted to wear diapers. That is a sad, lonely life to live. I hate to send these messages to other Adult Babies. The message I want to send to struggling Adult Babies is that you are worthy to live in this world, it is ok to be you, and you are entitled to live freely in this world! By staying hidden, I am sending the opposite message, which I consider to be negative, harmful, and psychologically damaging.

By living as my true self in everyday life, I experience true friends, true love, and inner peace. I also show other Adult Babies that it is ok to be who you are, no matter what everyone else says. I tell other Adult Babies "You are not alone", not in words, but in my actions. I tell the world that they can judge me if they want, but it will not change who I am, and I will not be bullied into submitting to your assigned character! I may inspire others to come out, and as our numbers grow, more Adult Babies will feel more confident in their actions to go public. In the future, it is possible that there will be no need to stay hidden at all.

*   *   *

Consider the lives homosexuals lived fifty years ago, and compare it to the lives they live today. I can't say it's *easy* to come out today as homosexual. They still have friends and family to face, and rejection to endure, but it is inarguably immensely easier than it was fifty years ago. Why? Well, we have the gay pioneers to thank. Harvey Milk was a great one, a hero of mine. Sean Penn stars in his biographical movie, which I recommend. There was also a documentary on Vito Russo, another great pioneer to the advancement of gay rights.

They, too, were told that their lifestyles were unacceptable, but they knew that they were who they were for a purpose, and refused to stay in the shadows! They went public despite being told of how inappropriate it was to be gay. What resulted? An entire gay rights movement. They faced the vulnerability of going public and the social attacks that transpired, and in doing so laid the groundwork for future generations to be openly gay, accepted for who they are, and live their lives to the fullest. Today, millions of homosexuals know "it's ok to be me" because Milk and Vito knew it in themselves fifty years prior.

Milk was shot and killed. I'm not saying there's no risk. We do live in a different, more open world today than we did in the 1960s, but as always, the choice is yours. Being yourself is never without risk, no matter who you are. It's just required for the truest happiness and the richest life livable.

Vito's main opponents came from within the LGBT community! It always amazes me that the greatest hatred we get for our differences are from people who have the same differences. Vito and Milk were both strongly criticized by the gay community for going public and "giving us all a bad name." At Vito's rallies, the flamers would fight with the butch gays, and the cross-dressers were attacked because they don't belong, and the lesbians are just freaks, so they don't belong, and it's thanks to the transgendered people that all homosexuals are labeled freaks in the first place. They hate each other more than they're hated by the populace. More accurately, they hated themselves. I believe the only reason they succeeded is because Vito called them out on it and lead them through it. He pointed out the absurdity of fighting amongst themselves when they all have the same goal: the freedom to live as themselves!

I experience this first-hand within the Adult Baby communities. I get far more hatred directed towards me from within the community than I do walking through the grocery store in my baby clothes. I mentioned my goals of being public, and they say I'm being all "in your face about it," and that I'm "giving all Adult Babies a bad name."

Being myself does not give another person a bad name. People will make connections and labels, but that does not make my expression of myself a bad thing.

*   *   *

Submitted for your approval: The true story of William Windsor.

William Windsor decided one day he would live his life as he was meant to be: as a baby girl. He would walk the streets of Phoenix wearing a baby-doll dress and thick diapers that everyone could see. His dolly was always in his hand. The adult William still came through at times. Yet, when he needed cigarettes, he'd stand in line at the 7-11 wearing his dress and diapers, and cuddling his doll.

It takes serious courage to live like that. He decided that he was sick of living as an imposter, and that he was going to live the life he was meant to live, damn the consequences! Admirable, no?

Apparently, no. Among the Adult Baby groups, this man is hated! The comments on YouTube videos featuring a 3-part news story on the baby girl (see web address in bibliography) suggest William to be a terrible man who "forces" this lifestyle on innocent bystanders. Really? Do straight people force their lifestyle on us when they hold hands in public? Do businessmen force their lifestyles on us by wearing ties publicly? If we can get past the social stigma, the ultimate truth is that we are who we are, we're all unique individuals, and we're all entitled to live our lives in this world as we see fit. Stop trying to control the harmless actions of others, and stop making the case that your life sucks because of what other people do! It's an excuse. You are in control of your own life, and you will make your own choices. Go public or don't. Let's not judge others for the choices they make.

*   *   *

As with the internal bickering among the LGBT community at Vito's rally, Adult Babies that bicker with other Adult Babies on how they live their own lives is rooted in insecurity. They crave the acceptance of others, and what others expect is for you not to be an Adult Baby. If they have to stay secret in their baby lives, then you should, too. I've said it before, and I'll say it again. All external judgment stems from self-judgment, and all external hatred stems from self-hatred. It is impossible to truly accept another person for exactly who they are if you can't accept yourself for who you are, and vice versa. A character expects other characters. Only the truly free can allow others to be truly free.

I urge Adult Babies to be more aware of this tendency to judge other Adult Babies. We are all on the same team! This constant bickering, judging, and condemning is causing only harm. Instead, let's focus on acceptance of others. To those of us that are able, let's rise above the bickering and set a finer example for the community and for the world.

THE DECISION IS UP TO YOU

The advice I offer is simply what worked for me. My authority on the subject was my amazing internal transformation from depressed to enlightened. This book is about how I made that transformation.

Will it work for everyone? I don't know. I'm certain my therapist is not as affective with others as with me. He spoke in a way that I could understand. The books I contribute to my transformation have not had the same effect on others I've recommended them to.

There is a specific time in a person's life that the message is needed, wherein he is not yet enlightened, but has become so miserable that they begin to crave and seek change. Those that are already enlightened don't need the help, and those that are comfortable in their uneasiness aren't yet ready for it.

Maybe I don't speak your language. The message I give may help one person out immensely, and confuse another even further.

It's also possible that we are all individuals with our own unique traits, needs, and views of the world. Each unique individual is meant to traverse a unique path of self-discovery. The things that worked for me may not work for everyone.

I write this section as if I could send it back in time to my younger self to read. When I was thirty and learned all this stuff that ended my perpetual depression, I wondered why this could be so obvious, yet nobody ever told me when I was younger! Ergo, I feel like the right thing to do is to spread the word. I am the first person to say that the message may not be for everyone.

So, yes! The decision is up to you. You must get to know yourself deeply. What do you need? Who are you on the deepest level? What is your purpose in life? What is best for you? What is stopping you? If it is the judgment you may face from others, that is a bad reason. If it's jail, well, that's a better reason. It may come down to how important it is to you.

I made my decision. I had beat depression and come a long way in my personal relationships, but I still found myself hiding my true self to the rest of the world. I reasoned that my true self would be offensive to others. Finally, I came to the conclusion that I am who I am, and nobody can change that. I was willing to face the hatred, abuse, and judgment rather than deny my soul free expression to the world.

And I did. I began living my life as I felt was comfortable. From then on, I could handle real rejection, rather than scenarios I make up in my head. But it was not the big deal I had imagined it to be. This was me. This was my decision.

Oddly, once I felt the freedom of being a toddler in public, the need was reduced greatly. After I went out in my baby clothes a few times, and I realized I was not trapped like I thought I was. Once I acquired the freedom, the need to be "out" was all but gone. Now, I live most of my life as an adult, but then again, I've always been more DL than AB. The trapped feeling exaggerates the need to fight restrictions. Once I learned I was not trapped, the needs subsided.

When we allow ourselves to release our repressed emotions, we often find them to vanish and outlive their purpose. To suggest that our AB tendencies are manifestations of repressed emotions is not a stretch by any means. It may play out that you give yourself the freedom to be yourself and express yourself as whom you are to the world without fear, and whom you are then changes and grows. You decide, one day, to go to the mall in your baby clothes, and enjoy the freedom. The next day, though, it doesn't seem so necessary. You decide in the morning that you will be yourself, but who you are has changed now that those repressed emotions have gotten their long awaited outlet. Now, to be yourself, maybe you don't need the baby clothes, as they have fulfilled their purpose. In this way, it is entirely possible that once you give yourself this freedom, you will no longer consider yourself an Adult Baby.

This is not the goal, mind you. Our goal is freedom, and should always be freedom. To stay hidden is to be a slave to society. However, to continue babyhood beyond its necessity is to be a slave to your own habits. Let's not get too attached to diapers and bottles. Be accepting of whatever comes. If you acquire the sought after freedom in your life, and your desires and needs for diapers and being babied fades, let it go. This is our inner evolution. If you acquire the freedom, and you still want to wear diapers and be babied, continue. Do it because you want to, not because you feel you have to. You may just trade one form of slavery for another.

Yes, once I gave myself the freedom of being myself anywhere I pleased, my desires faded. I know others whose desires increased. There is no right or wrong. It is just dangerous to become too identified with any act that we can't let it go. I no longer feel the compulsion to wear my baby clothes out.

Yet, there is a problem. The need is fading, yet I can't help but wear them all the time still. Why? Is it eight years of knowing nothing other than being diapered? Am I afraid to let that part of my life go? Do I consider myself an AB to the degree that if I were to let that go, I'd lose a part of myself? I am attached. This is my current struggle. I told you from the beginning that I did not have all the answers, I am not perfect, and I am a work in progress. But this book isn't about perfection. This book is about freedom to be yourself... your ever growing, constantly evolving self.

*   *   *

You are not trapped, except, perhaps, by your own mind. You have created scenario after scenario in your brain about what would happen if you lived how you've always dreamt of living, and the scenarios scare you into submitting to cultural standards of what's expected of you. Get past your mind, and recognize these scenarios as imaginary. Then experience real life for what it could be, and I assure you real life isn't as bad as what you've created in your mind. Even if it was, at least you'd be afraid of something real rather than imaginary. Otherwise, you'll live your entire life not knowing what it could be like. You'd be imagining what it could be like, but not knowing.

It's not our fault. We feel wrong. We are told by society or parents or peers that wearing diapers is wrong, yet there is something within ourselves that tell us that *not* wearing diapers feels so wrong. What results is a perpetual state of confliction; a damned if you do, damned if you don't scenario. No matter what we do, we feel wrong. Of our inner voices and the incoming voices (from parents/society/etc.), only one can be ignored.

So, it's not your fault you face this problem, but you do hold the solution. Whether this book helps you or not, this one fact applies to everyone: you hold the solution.

IT'S OK TO BE AN ADULT BABY

I can tell you this until I'm blue in the face, but it's no more meaningful than if anyone else were to tell you. For me, it's logical. We are more than our physical bodies. I've experienced this first hand, and so can you. That we exist gives us purpose. The purpose for our existence relies on our being ourselves; else we would have been created differently.

It may not make sense to you, and that's fine. This is not the sort of thing I could explain to another person. I am a finger pointing towards the moon. It must be experienced to be understood. Seek answers, and get to that point where you can believe with all of your heart that you are exactly who you are meant to be. It is not only ok to be you, it is required.

UNIVERSAL TO ALL

Fear is natural. If we are unhappy with the current situation, change is necessary. We fear change, and there is nothing wrong with that.

Fear is not a good reason to avoid doing something. Often, the fear tells us we're on the right track. We are taking on some vulnerability for the wonderful things that lie on the other side. Such is the importance of vulnerability. It is natural to fear vulnerability, yet vulnerability is a natural step to success of any kind.

Therefore, fear suggests vulnerability, and vulnerability suggests huge potential success. Fear is a reason to act!

*   *   *

Whenever you are planning to tell someone of your babyhood, ask yourself if you are seeking acceptance. In other words, how comfortable are you with the potential for rejection? We'll never be completely comfortable, but is it a simple risk/reward scenario to get to better things, or does our happiness hinge on their acceptance? If rejection will be devastating, you are not ready to tell, nor are you ready for relationships. You have much more self-examination to do.

It never gets completely easy. We're human, after all. Once we find ourselves, it takes practice, and becomes easier over time.

Your goal is not acceptance from others. Your ultimate goal is self-acceptance. All else will fall into place from there.

CUT PEOPLE SOME SLACK

I am the first to admit that a desire to wear diapers is very difficult to relate to. It is so weird, abnormal, rare, and bizarre, it is no wonder people don't understand. My parents didn't like to wear diapers. All they saw of Adult Babies was trashy daytime talk shows, which can be a poor representation of us. They are taught by society that different is wrong. When you attempt to sympathize with someone's difference, you imagine yourself in their position, or relate to something in your past. I could see how this could be trying when it comes to wearing diapers. This is a pretty strange thing we do, and as such would be difficult to relate to.

So, as frustrating as it is at times to be misunderstood, let's try to offer sympathy to those from whom we don't receive it. It's not easy to be an Adult Baby, but it's not easy to be human, either. Everyone struggles, and everyone tries to do the right things. You don't accept everyone you meet, as hard as you may try. Let's not judge others for their rejection of us. They, too, are people that aren't fully aware of the damage they can cause. To judge them causes only damage to ourselves.

FIND YOURSELF

I've repeated this exhaustively. It's not lack of substance. Rather, it's the importance of finding yourself.

Getting to know, love, and respect yourself goes a long way in the process of happiness as a person, much less an Adult Baby. This should be the main focus of your endeavor, before telling your loved ones, or before making any significant life changing decisions. Your first decision should be to learn to discover your true self. Meditate, get counseling, read The Power of Now, watch Kyle Cease videos on YouTube, do whatever it takes! Everybody's journey is different, yet entirely necessary.

You may need a map, but I assure you that you are the solution to all of your problems.

I wish you good luck. It is not easy being an Adult Baby. It is a difficult life, and there are many problems we have to deal with that many others would not understand. We also lack open communication to get help through these problems. I'm not a super-genius, and I'm not God. All I can offer is what worked for me, and what I believe can work for you. They are difficult things to implement into your life, especially if you have forgotten that you are an imposter and cannot imagine any other way, but they are worth it. Life is better than I ever could have imagined! You are capable of the same freedom others have, even if you are an Adult Baby. Want it, believe you are capable, and believe you deserve it. Face the fear, and great things will come of it.

Section 4:
Help! I'm living with an
Adult Baby!

It's not easy. You have done everything right; you have followed all the rules. All you've ever wanted was a normal, healthy life, and this is what you get?

These are the thoughts that run through your head when faced with a loved one professing to you that he wants to wear diapers.

The shock of abnormality will pass. It's not that big of a deal in the grand scheme of things. We have a culture that preaches an idea of normal. Normal is acceptable. Not normal, according to society, should be shunned. Society dictates what is acceptable and not acceptable. While this is a natural tendency of humankind, it's not real life.

In real life, the world is made up of a great number of individuals, each with his own mixture of traits. What society deems normal is merely the average. For example, many people have black hair; therefore, black hair is acceptable. Blue hair is unheard of, so when we are faced with a person who has blue hair, or God forbid, your teenager dyes his own hair blue, it is a shock. Not normal, not acceptable, not average.

This is all mere illusion, of course. Our brains have an appreciation for familiarity. Understandable, thinking in evolutionary terms. Humans have a certain level of survival programmed into their minds. Anything we have experienced already has not killed us, and is therefore safe. Anything that is new and unusual might kill us, and should be avoided, shunned, or even attacked. In modern times, we have trouble deciphering these life and death scenarios with silly social issues. It's natural, but obsolete.

Likewise, we want to fit in. Humans are social beings, and associate living in a pack with survival. Therefore, rejection equals ejection from the pack, which, millennia ago, would mean attempting lone survival, which would likely mean death. Again, this is obsolete today. Interesting, then, that we continue to crave social acceptance to the level we do. Our brains have not yet reached the level where rejection leads to anything aside from certain death, while socially this is no longer true.

So, rest assured, all the feelings you feel are natural, but may not be necessary in the current situation.

In reality, each and every person is unique; a precise mixture of millions of traits. Different hair color, skin color, music preferences, food preferences, dreams, desires, and personalities all make up who we are. They are an expression of nature. Call it God, evolution, Mother Nature, or the life force, the conclusion is the same. Each person is who they are meant to be. To reject a person is to reject reality.

Affection towards diapers, in reality, is no different than any other difference among us. Socially it's quite different, but we must remember that social standards are built upon averages from obsolete animalistic necessities.

We all deserve to live, flourish, prosper, and be happy. We are who we are. That is fact. You have no more or less right to be here and live your life than any other person you meet. To deny this right is to deny nature. It is akin to denying reality itself.

You are here to see and experience the world like no other person, past, present or future, ever possibly could. So why, then, would you deny yourself, or anyone else you meet, the right to live life the way they see fit?

I am aware that there comes a gray area when a person's path to happiness involves the destruction of another's, but this is not the case with Adult Babies. What harm is caused by wearing diapers, baby clothes, or acting like a toddler? Does it infringe on another person's right to happiness? It does not. One could make the argument that seeing your neighbor in a diaper is not appealing, but one could counter that your neighbor's purple car is hideous, and we circle back to obsolete societal standards.

One could also argue that wearing diapers is self-damaging. If, say, you were to allow your child to wear diapers, you'd be allowing him to live a difficult social life, where dating, working, and other social experiences become more difficult. This is true, to a point. It is difficult to live a healthy life in diapers, but I am proof that it is possible. What would be more damaging to your child is a parent that doesn't accept or love him for who he is. The greatest skill you could instill in your kin is the ability to respect and love himself for who he is. These social difficulties you base your denial on are paled in comparison. To deny one's true self in the name of social convenience may be the greatest moral crime one could commit.

Another argument you could make is the tons of pollution that go along with being diapered. This is no better a reason to deny the pleasure of diapers than to deny driving a car, enjoying a movie, or playing a computer game, all of which create pollution. Further, this is indirect harm, and difficult to measure accurately.

Morally speaking, my decision to wear diapers full time and enjoy my childhood well into my adult years has no negative impact on the people around me. Therefore, there is no moral ground to deny the pleasure.

Still, the more valid reasoning is that of our true being. Upon reading Section 2, you have learned that my obsession with diapers was not a choice. On the contrary, I attempted time and again to *choose* not to wear diapers. This was to no avail. I realize now that what I was attempting was to deny my true self. It didn't work for me, and it won't work for you, nor will it work for you forcing that denial on others.

What you will be faced with is a choice. You can accept the person in front of you for who he is, or you can choose to remove that person from your life (unless it's your minor child, of course). It is my opinion that to accept the person is the only righteous choice. To reject the person is to reject reality, which is ludicrous. I can promise that if you chose to reject the person, it is for the wrong reasons, as will be discussed. Lastly, you may be denying yourself a wonderful fulfilling relationship, and I would urge you to examine your reasons for doing so.

INSANE MYTH

It is a common conception that Adult Babies are mentally disturbed. Why else would an adult want to wet a diaper?

I must disagree. I am confident that I am not insane. I have had many healthy relationships and friendships, held many jobs, own my own business, have somehow managed to write a book, and my credit score is soaring. To be fair, I struggled with depression for decades, but this is a result of parental rejection rather than wearing diapers. I suppose you could suggest that the desire to wear diapers began with some sort of mental or emotional instability, but this would be pure conjecture, and an unfair assumption to make on a person.

Rather, the desire for diapers or babyish play is just a random trait someone can have. The reason it is thought of as crazy and instable is not because there are studies that suggest that Adult Babies are mentally instable. The only reason Adult Babies are thought of as crazy is because Adult Babies are rare. Rare equals abnormal, and abnormal equals unhealthy. Thus sayeth the mighty societal standards!

THE WRONG REASONS

The most common reason a person would reject an Adult Baby from being in his life is image. I see it all the time, and people are oblivious.

For instance, let's say you're married, and your spouse tells you of his diaper desires. What do you think? Well, after "he's insane" passes, then it goes to "what will my sister think?" or "what will the neighbors think?" In other words, the main thought is "How will my spouse being an Adult Baby reflect on ME?"

We all desire to be normal and accepted, and being an Adult Baby is neither. Being *married* to an Adult Baby, also, is neither. The fear sets in. "I have already failed in my attempt to be normal by dating someone that is abnormal."

Examine yourself. Why do you date? Is it to find someone you're happy with? Or is it to show off to all your friends what league you're in?

In another example, say your child has told you of his own desires to be diapered. What are your thoughts? First is probably "what did I do wrong?" The answer is nothing. People are who they are. You only have so much control over who your children turn out to be. Then your thoughts go to "What will the neighbors think?" Oh, and how they will talk at the next PTA meeting. "So-and-so's child is back in diapers? What terrible parents." Their judgment is meaningless. Their judgments are founded on social bullshit that exists only in their minds. Again, your thoughts go to how you will be perceived by others.

THE RIGHT REASONS

Maybe your desires are legitimate and healthy. What you seek in a relationship is someone with whom you can be happy. You have met the perfect person... Come to find out the perfect diapered person. Does that change who the person actually is? Will the interactions be different? Will the emotional support be different? If anything, they'd be deeper and more meaningful, as you are now included in his most intimate secret.

However, maybe diapers are disgusting to you. It could ruin the sexual relationship. Or you are just no longer attracted to the person. If these decisions are made thoughtfully, and are not about what others think - or image - it would not be unreasonable to break off the relationship.

I am not going to tell you that dating an Adult Baby is the right decision, while denying them is wrong. I am not you. You have your own standards, desires, and dreams. You should know what's right for you better than I. The choice is yours. Just make the best choice for you, personally. What others will think of your decision should not sway you.

STINKING MYTH

"But I don't want a stinky boyfriend!"

This one always makes me laugh. Some of the more offensive people will say that Adult Babies "walk around all day carrying a load in their pants."

Not true. I do not stink. Well, after the gym, maybe. Being an Adult Baby does not make you inept at self-hygiene. In making your decision to be or not to be in a relationship, perhaps you should ask questions about what, exactly, they do. Section 1 teaches us that each Adult Baby is different, and assumptions should not be made. Do they like stinky diapers? Do they use their diapers? Perhaps they do enjoy carrying a load in their pants all day long. Denying a relationship on hygiene is reasonable. Presuming Adult Babies have poor hygiene is not.

I use my diapers often, but only number one, as is my personal preference. I live a healthy daily life with nary an offensive odor. My coworkers have no idea I'm wearing wet diapers at the end of the day. My girlfriends have never complained. I provide the respect of showering before our intimate times, as should we all. The majority of AB-related reasons girls have denied dating me have been unfounded. You must get to know your Adult Baby well to make an informed decision.

HELP! MY SPOUSE IS AN ADULT BABY!

Rough spot to be in. I can't blame you too much. It is every person's responsibility to show his true self in a relationship, most certainly before any proposal or wedding. It's difficult to be in a committed relationship and learn that the person to whom you're committed is not who you thought he was. I sympathize.

How did you get into this predicament anyway? I have a theory on healthy relationships. Both parties must provide openness, honesty, and acceptance. Acceptance holds in it a certain level of approachability. That is to say that, if every time your partner says something you're uncomfortable with you scream at him, he will refrain from telling you uncomfortable things in the future. One's lack of acceptance discourages the other's openness and honesty. It is basic human nature. So, if you've not been the most approachable person in the past, perhaps this is an area for improvement.

Still, the majority of blame falls on the Adult Baby. Even without the approachability, as difficult as it may be, the openness and honesty is still required. It's your duty in a relationship.

All this is moot now. You're already married, and he's "coming out". My first advice is to stay calm. Breathe. This is not the end of the world. Your spouse is still who your spouse has always been. You are just learning of another trait. This does not make him insane. Look deep inside yourself to remind yourself that what others think of you does not truly affect you.

Your spouse is providing honesty for you. That is what healthy relationships are. You want a fulfilling relationship, and you want honesty. Consider why he's kept it secret, and thank him for being honest. Do not react angrily. Breathe deep. You may need some time to process this information.

What you don't want to do is react immediately with anger. If you shout, you're telling your spouse not to say anything that is discomforting in this relationship. This can contradict your desire for honesty. Do not criticize or name-call. This person is as God has made him. No point in denying it, right?

That's what it all comes down to: acceptance of who we are. If you reject a person's diaper compulsions, you are rejecting the person. If you reject who the person is, you are rejecting reality! It is completely unproductive.

You may consider counseling, but for what? If it's to get him to stop, forget it. He may or may not, but if he were to quit for you, it would be for the wrong reasons, and will not result in a healthy relationship. If it's to examine why he had such trouble telling you, or why you hate him so much for it, and to filter through all the emotions, that could be a valuable reason for counseling.

I am speaking from my own, very personal experience. I did not choose to have this diaper obsession. I did choose to live out these incredibly strong desires by wearing diapers, but it was hardly a choice as the desire was so intense. Nobody could make me stop but me, and I will only do so because it benefits me personally. I couldn't do it for anyone else, or it would be hollow, and doomed to relapse.

I am not crazy. If I was crazy, I doubt I'd know it, so it's silly for me to even make that claim. The reason I do so, though, is to inform you that Adult Babies are not crazy across the board. We are but mere people, with the same needs and desires as everyone else, and equally deserving of love and respect. I do not make these pleas for myself, but for the other Adult Babies in the world.

My point, I guess, is to encourage you to understand the situation. Who you are, who your spouse is, what makes your spouse want to be babied, etc. Drop the worries of what others will think of you, and ignore your assumptions on the situation.

Then, if you have decided that you will not be happy with an Adult Baby, keeping in mind that you married him, and that this single trait is something that you refuse to accept despite his other qualities for which you married him, and you know exactly why you refuse to accept the trait, and are morally okay with that, AND you feel strongly enough that it outweighs the sanctity of your wedding vows, (AND, if you have kids, you are willing to let them grow up with separated parents), then by all means, seek divorce.

Probably a better way to handle it is to accept your spouse as the amazing person you married. You learn more about each other each day. That never ends! So why should this be any different? Whether you want to be a part of his AB life or not is a different matter, but don't rule it out so quickly. I would hope that you would jump at any chance you get to become more intimate with your lover. If not, then I must wonder why you got married in the first place.

There is a fine line between expanding your comfort zone, and abandoning it. You don't want to do something you are completely uncomfortable with, but to remain within your comfort zone is to remove any potential for growth. Expand your comfort zone, gently and gradually, while staying true to yourself.

What you do with your own life, however, is up to you. I certainly don't advise sacrificing your own happiness for your spouse's, nor would I advise the same for your spouse. There must be a balance if you want the relationship to work. Since you've gotten married, it is my opinion that you owe the effort. I believe you would expect the same from him.

HELP! MY CHILD WANTS DIAPERS!

Stay calm. Don't react emotionally immediately. The world is not ending. You've done nothing wrong. Everything will be ok. Don't panic.

Your child is not insane, mentally ill, or crazy.

You want what is best for your child. It would be wise to take some time examining this issue to determine the best course for action.

Once you have taken the time to calm down and soak it all in, we can move ahead and start solving some problems.

To get the fullest understanding of a child that wants to wear diapers, you must read this book in its entirety. This section, while direct, will not provide the full picture. Reading through Section 2, for instance, will give valuable insight into what may be going on in your child's mind, as well as the potential influence your decisions have over your child's future.

*   *   *

First, what is the problem? A child wearing a diaper is, at its core, harmless. Yet, it doesn't feel harmless. Why? Are you concerned with his mental health? Are you concerned with what the neighbors will think? Are you worried that your child will not find his place in a society containing certain expectations of him? Or, perhaps, you feel like you've done something wrong as a parent. Find the basis of your concern and you will see that it is, in fact, nominal. The very act of wearing a diaper, in itself, is completely harmless.

Each parent has a responsibility to love and respect their child for exactly who he is. Often, parents believe their responsibility lies in determining who their child becomes, but parents don't always have that control over their children. Identical twins do not have identical personalities. Why not? They were raised the same and are genetically identical, so why the difference? There is something within each of us that determines who we are and who we become beyond genetics, and beyond nurture. The truth is that much of who a child becomes is outside of the parents' circle of influence. A child comes to this world not from his parents, but *through* his parents.

This is not easy for parents to accept. We feel that if our children were to take on characteristics we don't like, or we don't think is good for them, it is our fault for not raising them properly. Often, decisions parents make are not in the best interest of the child, but the best interest of the parents.

Our responsibility as parents is not to control who our children become, but to nourish and guide our children to become the best adults they can be. It is difficult to decipher the difference, but the answer lies in acceptance. No matter your approach to parenting, the love and acceptance of your children must be unconditional.

Fact: Your child is who he is. As a parent, you must accept him as he is. To deny your child is to deny reality.

A child needs his parents' love and acceptance. If a child expresses himself, and the parents make it clear that who he is is not acceptable, the child will live as a character he creates in order to receive the love and acceptance he requires. He will grow up unaware of who he truly is, and suffer emotionally for it.

Specifically, your child wants to wear diapers. If you were to tell him that wanting to wear diapers is wrong, he will feel like his emotions are wrong and suppress them. A new character will emerge, one that does not want to wear diapers, so his parents will accept him. The desire to wear diapers hasn't gone away, but was repressed. His own feelings and desires have been invalidated by his parents. This will cause major emotional damage in his life, even through adulthood, until he learns to love himself for who he is. I hit this milestone at age thirty, and I believe I was ahead of the curve. Some hit it earlier, and others never do.

You may tell your child that wearing diapers is bad, but it would be a lie. It may be your opinion, or that you don't allow it, or that he's an abomination. These will not end his desires, but will make him feel guilty, or like an abomination. The desires will not go away, but he will be conflicted between his own desires and the love and acceptance of his parents. I'd also suggest that if you think that wearing a diaper is wrong, but committing your child to a lifetime of depression is acceptable, you must rethink your moral values.

Now, I'm not saying you must allow your child to wear diapers. You must, however, accept your child for who he is and respect his feelings and desires. Denying his feelings does not make them go away. It suppresses his feelings and causes terrible emotional problems for him as he grows into an adult. You, as a parent, have a responsibility. Accept your child for who he is, and relinquish control over who he becomes.

*   *   *

Often, parents take issue with our child's actions not because they are directly harmful to the child, but because they may reflect poorly on the parents themselves.

Ask yourself why you have a problem with your child or teen wearing diapers. Do you feel like you've done something wrong? I would doubt that you did. I do not feel like I was fixated on diapers at age three because of something my parents did. I could be wrong. If it were a result of something my parents did, I am sure it was not intentional. Why I would want to wear diapers at three is not the question. It is common to look at the reasons behind why we got into the situations in which we find ourselves. We figure the answers to how to handle the problem will surface if we find the cause of the problem. This is not necessarily the case. The solution to our problems surface when we merely accept the problem as it is. Often, finding the cause proves elusive and an utter waste of time. Instead, focus on accepting the current situation.

Why does your child want to wear diapers? Why probably does not matter. I've heard stories of children that have bladder control issues, and they don't know how to express what's happening in their bodies, so they just ask for diapers. It's worth checking out, but this was not the case for me. If the reason is psychological, finding out why is at best unnecessary, and at worst and endless chase that will end in an answerless frustration. Rather, accept it.

"Accept that my potty trained child wants to wear diapers?" Yes. You must not take so much responsibility for who your kin has become. Your kid is an expression of nature, a being of his own life-force, a unique individual. Your child didn't come from you as much as *through* you.

Allow for him to be his own person with his own collection of traits. Accept it. Who your child has become is exactly who he is meant to be. To deny your child is to deny reality.

"What will the neighbors think?" It doesn't matter. Let them think what they think. To live by another's standards is to value who *they* think your child *should* be over his true self.

"What does this mean about me as a parent?" Nothing. Your child is who he is. If you had control over who your kids became, then each family would have identical children. You'd be the same as your siblings, your parents are the same as your aunts and uncles, identical twins are identical in personalities as well, etc. It is a fact that much of who your child is was never in your circle of influence. The test of your parenting skills is not in who your child has become, but how you handle raising him now.

Remember that as a parent, it is your job to accept him and love him for who he is. The gut feeling from a parent's perspective may be that if you were to allow your child to wear diapers, you'd be signing him up for a lifetime of social awkwardness. Arguable, but let's assume it's true. I can certainly say that a parent's rejection will be far more damaging.

Parents have trouble foreseeing a healthy adult life that involves diapers. What they fail to see is that the absence of parental approval is far more harmful to a child's psyche than any diaper could ever be. Let me be an example of a healthy adult with a healthy life as an Adult Baby.

I'd have been much better off with my parents providing unconditional love and letting me wear diapers. What I got was verbal abuse and a ban on diapers. The rejection is what caused all my psychological problems through my teens and twenties, not the diapers.

The irony is that even with my parents refusing to allow me to wear diapers, it didn't really stop me. I never magically became normal. The desire for diapers never left. I'd just sneak the diapers when I could. When I became an adult and could make my own choices, buying adult diapers was choice number one! My parents' attempt at control did result in guilt, low self-esteem, self-hatred, and depression. They were trying to fix something that wasn't broken, and caused far deeper problems than they were trying to prevent.

Ignoring the problem will not make it go away. Denying your child the right to wear diapers will not make your child normal, nor will it drive away the desires. In fact, the denial may *increase* the child's fixation on diapers. The deepest parts of us we deny will always fight back in greater force.

Parents often don't see the big picture. Parents try to do the right thing and don't see the damage they're causing.

I am speaking from my own experience. I am assuming that your child is like me, obsessed with diapers from a very young age, feeling alone, different, unlovable, and confused. The fixation on diapers was ingrained in my being. Nobody in the world could have "cured" me of it, because it was not a disease, but a part of me. You know how my parents handled the situation having read

Section 2, and you know the damage it caused. I am offering an alternative that will result in much healthier and productive children once adulthood is reached. That they wear diapers under their clothes is far less significant than we believe it to be. The health of our souls, however, holds all the importance in the world.

Maybe your child is not like me. Maybe the diaper interest is not so deeply ingrained, but a general curiosity. How would you handle the situation then? How would you even know the difference? To make a good decision, you must know the situation well. This can be easily accomplished with a good conversation between you and your offspring. There are rules, though. Openness, honesty, and your particular job in this case: acceptance. You must be willing to accept your child for exactly who he is. You cannot get frustrated or angry, or you will scare him from telling you the truth, or maybe he'll feel like it's wrong to be him. When accurately identified, these negative feelings, you will find, are not directed towards your child, but towards yourself. Work through them on your own. They are not meant to be directed outward.

I felt like a bad person for most of my life for something that was beyond my control. This is not something you want to instill on your child.

If your child is not so enamored with diapers as I was, then I leave the decision up to you. (Well, all the decisions are up to you.) You can let them explore, or you can tell them you'd prefer it if they didn't. If their interest persists, reassess. Do not get in the habit of ignorance. It may be bliss for you, but it is not for your child.

*   *   *

What if you just found diapers in your kid's room? Well, first I commend you for reading this book. It is a wise step towards understanding your child, and that you want to understand him says a lot about you as a parent.

Don't be angry. Kids lie because they feel like they're doing something wrong. Often, what we consider "wrong" is simply not normal. What they fear is parental rejection. What is more important is *why* they lied. There really is only one reason to lie in a relationship, and that is lack of approachability. If you want your children to be honest with you, you must control your reactions. Yelling, screaming, and punishment are terrible reactions to your child expressing himself. Lead his behavior with gentle guidance, but don't control his being. It is not always easy for a parent to decipher between the two.

Have a good talk with your kid, and open up a line of communication that, judging by the hidden diapers, is currently closed. Your kid will appreciate it more than anything, and it will most certainly result in a healthier adult.

*   *   *

I cannot tell you how to raise your kids. All I can do is bring to your attention the damage certain actions may cause, and the help the right actions can provide. It's a matter of general attitude more than specific actions. Love and acceptance are entirely necessary. Understand that they probably do not choose to have the desires they have. It confuses them far more than it could confuse you. It is not an easy life to grow up knowing that you're different than everyone else, feeling like you're alone in the world. These are the types of things that may be going on in your child that you do have control over.

It's pure conjecture, but if I had received the unconditional love and acceptance I deserved, I am sure that I'd have become a healthier adult. I also believe that, had I been allowed to wear diapers early on in life, like at age four around when I first remember the desires, the fixation would not have taken such a strong hold on me.

What ifs are as useless as whys, though. What matters is that I was who I was, and I am who I am, you are who you are, and your kid is who he is. The sooner we can accept these facts, the better off we all are. There are some things about people that are beyond your control.

*   *   *

This concludes the section on parenting, yet I have not directly told you to allow your children to wear diapers, or to deny them the right. This is not my decision to make. I believe that commonly, allowing a potty trained child to wear unneeded diapers would be considered bad parenting, and I offer a differing opinion, yet I have not offered explicit instructions on what to allow or restrict your child from doing.

In the end, I believe that whether you allow or disallow your child to wear diapers pales in comparison to the importance of accepting your child. It is true that the level of acceptance you offer your child will sway your decisions regarding what you allow your child to do. Ultimately, this book is not about allowing your child to wear diapers or not. This section is about being the best parent you can be, and giving your diaper-loving child the best life he can acquire. I believe that the advice in this section, if properly valued, will achieve just that.

A final piece of advice: <u>Drama of a Gifted Child</u>, by Alice Miller, depicts well the emotional needs of the children, and the difficulties parents have in providing those needs. If you struggle to accept your child as is, it is, most likely, rooted in a struggle to accept yourself. This relatively short book will help.

*   *   *

Maybe you have read earlier my suggestion that your kids lie to you about needing diapers. Maybe this angers you, but it need not. If you are welcoming and accepting of your child, and if you love your child no matter what, then I am not talking to your child. If you freak out and become abusive because your child wants to wear diapers, then you are in need of some schooling, and until you have reached the next level, I stand by my suggestion that your child to lie to you. Every relationship requires honesty and acceptance. The two go hand in hand. If you don't provide acceptance, you will certainly not receive any form of honesty. End of story.

ADULT BABIES IN SOCIETY

I have covered what to do in situations where your spouse or child is an ABDL. I think these are the only two really significant situations that would demand a serious level acceptance. Any advice for a spouse can be applied to a boyfriend or girlfriend, the difference being a lack of vows. For a person accepting a friend, sibling, or roommate, I couldn't imagine offering any advice I haven't already given in the past two sections.

There are some thoughts I have on the general opinion of Adult Babies I'd like to address, though.

It is bothersome to me that most of the populace gets their exposure to Adult Babies on trashy talk shows. These talk shows are a poor representation of *any* subculture. Generally speaking, the shows' producers do not find the best representative of a subculture, but the most shocking of a subculture to shock their audience and get them talking, achieving higher Nielson ratings.

Among Adult Baby groups, there seems to be a consensus, albeit a misguided one, that Adult Babies should stay private, as going public gives us all a bad name. Nothing could be further from the truth.

I offer the opposing view that staying private is precisely what gives us the bad name. First, it leaves public exposure limited to the weirdoes that the talk shows find. (It is true that not *all* ABDLs on talk shows are weirdoes.) Second, by hiding, we are telling the world that we have something to hide. Third, it goes against a core value of mine: You are meant to be and live as exactly who you are. Fourth, one person going public says nothing about another member who's remained private. This fear that the Adult Babies that go public give us as a community a bad name is based on a lack of self-acceptance, and an overvaluation of the opinions of others.

While, admittedly, it is partially our fault as Adult Babies, society tends to fear us far more than need be. Society looks upon Adult Babies as creepy, weird, unhealthy, mentally instable, perverted, or pedophiles.

The last things we're considered is people, cohabitants of the world, or fellow citizens.

It's a cycle. Adult Babies stay private, giving society the appearance of rarity. Society is left to make its own assumptions on us, tending towards judgment. Rare is bad, after all. The judgment we face from society keeps us hidden, and staying hidden leaves society to assume.

I encourage society to be more accepting of others for their differences, and I encourage the community to be more open with their own differences. But I have no control over other people. The greatest influence I have is to live my life in the way I believe best benefits me and the world.

This opinion is not without its opponents. Within the Adult Baby community, people fear me. It's private, they say, and should remain so. In general society, there are those that feel being openly AB is inappropriate, and should not be tolerated.

In either case, the reasons are poor, and deny one's individuality and freedom to express self.

I would like to see the AB community follow in the footsteps of homosexuals. A mere fifty years ago they were judged, beaten, abused, discriminated, and denied basic human rights. They gathered together and went public, damn the consequences. Oh, how I admire their courage.

Nowadays, they have become more and more accepted. Society is not without its haters - nor will it ever be - but homosexuals are generally accepted.

Accepting homosexuals into society is thought of as even admirable now. Why, then, do we continue to reject other subcultures for their differences?

Says the hyper-intelligent former U.S. congressman Ron Paul, "The misunderstanding that tolerance is an endorsement of certain activities motivates many to legislate moral standards..." This was in reference to federal law, but his insight into tolerance is invaluable. Tolerance is across the board, or it is not tolerance at all, but an "endorsement of certain activities." Accepting homosexuality is becoming easier and easier because it is becoming more and more normal! The purest form of tolerance, however, is universal. Accept every individual for their unique collection of traits handed to them by God.

We are all different. There's no argument. No two people in the world are the same. Why, then, are we so quick to shun those that are different from us? We all carry with us secrets, yet we all judge others for theirs. We fear being our true selves, but judge others for being theirs. The egoistic part of us that judges others is the same part that judges our own self. When we each learn our place in the world, the importance of others living under our own rules evaporates into the ether. You are free to be you, I am free to be me, and the same goes for each unique individual, regardless of their quirks.

Contact

If you'd like to contact me to further discuss the matters in this book, please email me at brianman3@yahoo.com.

Bibliography

1. <u>The Power of Now</u>, Eckhart Tolle, 2004.
2. <u>Change your thoughts- Change your life: Living the Wisdom of the Tao</u>; Dr. Wayne Dyer, reprint edition 2009.
3. <u>Drama of a Gifted Child: The Search for the True Self</u>, Alice Miller, revised edition, 1996.
4. William Windsor; Phoenix channel three local news story;
   - Video one of three YouTube link: http://youtu.be/x_5Wduvq9pc
   - Video two of three YouTube link: http://youtu.be/Pz4TnNA_jdI
   - Video three of three YouTube link: http://youtu.be/ecSzZfXRH44
5. Kyle Cease YouTube videos;
   - Evolving out loud: http://youtu.be/rA3x8gA7rY4
   - Drop your addictions: http://youtu.be/YZ-DMs1iMb0
   - How to let go of people's opinions and get in the flow: http://youtu.be/mLCjlTkn87w
6. <u>Awaken the Giant Within: How to Take Control of Your Immediate Mental, Emotional, Physical, and Financial Destiny!,</u> Anthony Robbins, 2007.

7. Reference to cloned cow experiment;
    http://www.technologyreview.com/view/411834
    /the-dark-side-of-pet-cloning/

Made in the USA
San Bernardino, CA
02 June 2015